Why You Can Disagree...
and Remain a Faithful Catholic

In fide, unitas; in dubiis, libertas; in omnibus, caritas.
In faith, unity; in doubtful matters, liberty; in all things, love.
—ATTRIBUTED TO ST. AUGUSTINE OF HIPPO—

New York Times/CBS News Poll, August 24, 1986*

The poll shows widespread disagreement with official Roman Catholic teaching on issues of birth control, divorce/remarriage, and abortion. Yet most Catholics feel they can hold their positions and still remain good Catholics.

What American Catholics Think (%)			
	All Ages	Age 18–39	Age 40+
Favor use of artificial birth control	68	83	51
Oppose	24	11	38
Favor allowing Catholics divorce/remarriage	73	80	63
Oppose	19	13	27
Favor legal abortion	26	37	13
Only to save mother or in rape/incest cases	55	49	63
Oppose	15	10	20
Can disagree with pope on these issues and be good Catholic	79	86	71
Cannot disagree	13	12	16

---

*A 1987 poll taken just before the papal visit to the United States showed a slight increase in support for the official teaching on artificial birth control and divorce and remarriage. There was a slight increase among those who would not permit any abortions and those who would support legal abortion. The question about disagreeing with the pope was not included (*New York Times,* September 10, 1987).

Why You Can Disagree...
and Remain a Faithful Catholic

PHILIP S. KAUFMAN, O.S.B.

A Meyer-Stone Book
CROSSROAD • NEW YORK

1994

The Crossroad Publishing Company
370 Lexington Avenue, New York, NY 10017

Cover design: Jantina Eshleman

Typesetting output: T$_E$XSource, Houston

Manufactured in the United States of America

Library of Congress Cataloging in Publication Data

Kaufman, Philip S., 1911–
  Why you can disagree—and remain a faithful
Catholic.

  Includes index.
  1. Catholic Church—Doctrines.   2. Catholic
Church—Infallibility.   I. Title.
BX1751.2.K335   1989   282   88-43051
ISBN 0-940989-23-9

Contents

Chronology

1073–1085	Pope St. Gregory VII — celibacy of clergy
1159–1181	Pope Alexander III — marriage reform
1198–1216	Pope Innocent III — papal "fullness of power"
1220–1254	Holy Roman Emperor Frederick II and the Papacy
1243–1254	Pope Innocent IV
1245	Deposition of Frederick
1294–1303	Pope Boniface VIII and Philip IV (the Fair)
1295–1350	Conflict between of Church and State
1438–1445	Council of Florence — attempted reunion with Greeks
1517	BEGINNING OF PROTESTANT REFORMATION
1545–1563	Council of Trent — reforming Catholic council
1793–1873	FRENCH REVOLUTION AND THE NAPOLEONIC ERA
1846–1878	Pope Pius IX — *Tuas libenter* (1863), Syllabus of Errors
1869–1870	Vatican Council I — *Pastor aeternus,* papal infallibility defined
1903–1914	Pope Pius X — biblical decrees on scripture
1922–1939	Pope Pius XI — *Casti connubii,* on marriage (1930)
1939–1958	Pope Pius XII — *Humani generis* (1950)
1958–1963	Pope John XXIII — opening of Vatican Council II
1962–66	VATICAN COUNCIL II
1963–1978	Pope Paul VI — *Humanae vitae,* on birth control (1968)
1978–	Pope John Paul II
1980	International Synod of Bishops on the Family
1987	International Synod of Bishops on the Laity

Foreword

One of the anomalies of Catholicism is the coexistence of two phenomena: a faith and trust in the enlightening and guiding presence of the Holy Spirit to the church, including individual believers, and yet an apparent distrust of the free flow of ideas in the church. Thus, for example, as recently as 1987 Pope John Paul II stated that the church's teaching on contraception is not a matter of free theological discussion. That statement is not the result of broad consultation with theologians, priests, and laypeople. The Holy Father's phraseology, taken literally from Pius XII's encyclical *Humani generis*, is theologically tricky and not without the need for interpretation. But its overall public impact is the provision of support to those who discredit any expression of dissenting opinion in the church as illegitimate or worse. That is when the Holy Spirit is sent packing.

Philip Kaufman, rightly I am convinced, will have none of this. Catholics, he argues, have a right to know not only official teaching, but also "other information in the church." He borrows this from the distinguished moral theologian Bernard Häring, who stated in the wake of *Humanae vitae:*

> Those who are doubtful whether they can accept it have to study it thoroughly, have to read it with good will, but they also have to accept other information in the church. They cannot dissociate the pope from the whole of the church. They have to study it, consider it, but not alone, not isolated.

Kaufman's book is, in a sense, an expansion of that "other information" on several burning issues. He first presented us with the central theme of this book in an article in *Commonweal* (September 12, 1980) entitled "An Immoral Morality?" in which he rejected as immoral an imposition of obligations that discounted theological opinion in the church. When the article appeared I reviewed it in "Notes on Moral Theology" (*Theological Studies,* March 1981). I wrote:

When dissent occurs against an official formulation and becomes "massive" throughout the Church, it cannot be viewed as "isolated speculation" with no relationship to practical everyday living. That is exactly what Häring and Kaufman are underlining. To say anything different is to put truth in the service of authority and official formulations. It should be exactly vice versa.

Kaufman knows very well that there are powerful forces at work in the church attempting to reduce the reflections in his book to "isolated speculation." That is why his study is a courageous one — an odd adjective, one would think, to have to use in our day. Yet it remains apropos. For when the official attempt to achieve uniformity stumbles at the bar of experience and ideas, the next step is to disenfranchise the speculator.

The price of that step can be steep, as Kaufman makes clear in the final paragraphs of his book. One can disagree with this or that sentence, this or that analysis in Kaufman's study. Indeed, his own attitude and principles toward "other information" warmly invite such responses as part of the ongoing teaching-learning process of a pilgrim church. What one cannot do with historical or theological support is to dismiss the idea that there legitimately *can be* "other information" or that it is of continuing relevance, even urgency, in the church. And that is the idea that generates and organizes this thoughtful book. It is why it should be studied carefully.

RICHARD A. MCCORMICK, S.J.
John A. O'Brien Professor of Christian Ethics
University of Notre Dame

Preface

On the one hand and on the other hand!
— *Fiddler on the Roof*

In matters of morality, the Roman Catholic church tends to speak inconsistently to its members. At times, it emphasizes the role of conscience in decision making. The American bishops have stated that our spiritual tradition accepts "enlightened conscience, even when honestly mistaken, as the immediate arbiter of moral decision."[1] Presumably, therefore, Catholics have the right to know legitimate options in order to make enlightened decisions on controverted moral issues.

Yet the Roman magisterium, that is, the teaching authority of the Catholic church in Rome, issues authoritative statements on specific moral issues, statements that, as Karl Rahner has said, "can make no claim to be definitive" and yet "are nonetheless presented in such a way as though in fact they are definitive."[2]

To deprive Catholics of the knowledge of legitimate choices in their moral decision making, to insist that moral issues are closed when actually they are still open, is itself immoral. Likewise, according to Bernard Häring, "one of the most influential Catholic moral theologians of our century,"[3] "to allow others to manipulate one's conscience" sins against liberty and sanity.[4]

Moreover, the problem extends beyond the church's own members to the ecumenical dialogue. Again, speaking of Protestant difficulties with the pope's role as teacher in the church, Rahner wrote:

> On the one hand, the ordinary teaching office of the pope, at least in its authentic doctrinal decisions, often contains

---

[1] *Human Life in Our Day*, a collective pastoral letter of the American hierarchy, issued on November 15, 1968, at their annual meeting in Washington, D.C., no. 43.

[2] Karl Rahner, "Open Questions in Dogma Considered by the Institutional Church as Definitively Answered," *Journal of Ecumenical Studies*, vol. 15, no. 2 (Spring 1978), p. 212.

[3] *America*, vol. 156, no. 17 (May 2, 1987), p. 362.

[4] Bernard Häring, *General Moral Theology*, vol. 1, *Free and Faithful in Christ: Moral Theology for Clergy and Laity* (New York: Seabury, 1978), p. 263.

errors, even up to our own day; and secondly, Rome normally presents and pushes doctrinal decisions that are *per se* reformable as though there were no doubt whatsoever about their definitive correctness and as though further discussion about the matter by Catholic theologians would be inappropriate.[5]

Whether our concern lies with the consciences of Roman Catholics or with relations between the Roman Catholic church and other Christian bodies, Rome's teaching authority is, therefore, of critical importance. Sometimes Rome teaches reformable doctrines as if they were definitively closed, seeking to apply "the cloak of infallibility" to teachings that have not been formally defined. Catholics as well as Protestants have been led to believe that many open issues have been infallibly decided. So before addressing specific concrete questions we will, in chapter 1, look at the whole notion of infallibility. We will see that official Catholic teaching on the issues I have chosen to deal with — birth control, divorce and remarriage, intercommunion[6] — cannot justifiably be designated as defined, that is, infallibly taught.

In chapter 2, we will speak of "probabilism," an important resource in the Catholic moral tradition. According to probabilism, when genuine uncertainty exists about a precept's obligatory nature, the conscientious believer may justifiably follow a minority, "probable" opinion of competent theologians.

Chapters 3–7 apply insights on infallibility and probabilism to concrete issues in Christian lives. Birth control is discussed in Chapters 3–5. Chapters 6–7 consider divorce and remarriage.

Underneath all discussion of decisions of conscience lies the question: How is God's will made known in the church? Since, according to Vatican II, God "distributes special graces among the faithful of every rank" (*Lumen gentium,* no. 12), God's will may be made known through the whole church. Chapters 8–9, on "Democracy in the Church," explore this issue, particularly in relation to the question of intercommunion.

To be authentically Roman Catholic it is not enough to be Roman, to listen only to the Vatican. It is also necessary to be

---

[5]"Open Questions in Dogma Considered by the Institutional Church as Definitively Answered," p. 221.

[6]For abortion, see my article "Abortion: Catholic Pluralism and the Potential for Dialogue," *Cross Currents,* vol. 37, no. 1 (Spring 1987), pp. 76–86.

catholic, to consider many ways, past and present, in which the
Spirit has guided and continues to guide the church to truth.
History is a great liberator and a recourse to history often helps
us resolve problems in our own day. We need knowledge of the
church's wider history, both past and present, to make conscientious decisions.

Bernard Häring, a member of Pope Paul's "birth control"
commission, spoke at Holy Cross Abbey, Canon City, Colo.,
shortly after promulgation in 1968 of the encyclical *Humanae
vitae*. In his talk Häring showed Catholics how to form their
consciences in view of the encyclical's prohibition of all artificial contraception. He emphasized that no one need leave the
church because of inability to follow the pope's teaching:

> Those who are doubtful whether they can accept it have
> to study it thoroughly, have to read it with good will, but
> they also have to accept other information in the church.
> They cannot dissociate the pope from the whole of the
> church. They have to study it, consider it, but not alone,
> not isolated.

This book seeks to provide some of the "other information."

The many participants in my adult education classes de-
serve much credit for my growth in understanding of the issues
treated here. Other individuals who have been particularly help-
ful include, from St. John's University, Thomas L. Amos, Hill
Monastic Manuscript Library; Alfred Deutsch, O.S.B.; Carmela
Franklin; the late Ivan Havener, O.S.B.; John Kulas, O.S.B.;
Aaron Raverty, O.S.B.; Martin Schirber, O.S.B.; Robert Spaeth,
formerly Dean of the College of Arts and Sciences; and Daniel
Ward, O.S.B.; and also Linda Mealey, College of St. Benedict;
Paul Hammer, Colgate-Rochester Divinity School; Theodore
Mackin, S.J., Santa Clara University; James A. Brundage,
University of Wisconsin-Milwaukee; Andrew Greeley, National
Opinion Research Center, University of Chicago; Joseph De-
Santo, Iona College; Raymond C. Schulze, Immanuel Lutheran
Church, New York City; and Robert Blair Kaiser. A special
word of thanks is due to the reference staffs of the libraries of
St. John's University and of Iona College. John Eagleson, ed-
itorial director of Meyer-Stone Books, more than anyone else,
is responsible for the book's unity and coherence. I want to

thank him publicly for excellent, active editorial work. Without Dave Meyer's prodding the book would never have been written. I accept, however, full responsibility for what I have written.

Chapter 1

Teaching Infallibly in the Church

No doctrine is understood to be infallibly defined unless it is clearly established as such.
— *Code of Canon Law*

On August 18, 1986, Father Charles E. Curran, highly respected professor of moral theology at the Catholic University in Washington, D.C., received from Cardinal Joseph Ratzinger, prefect of the Congregation for the Doctrine of the Faith, a letter that had been approved by Pope John Paul II. The letter, dated July 25, stated that Curran was "no longer considered suitable or eligible to exercise the function of a Professor of Catholic Theology."[1]

Two days later a front-page story in the *New York Times* read: "Ban on Priest Is Said to Define Moral Teachings as Infallible." According to the story, silencing Curran had wide implications. The *Times* reported:

An official familiar with Cardinal Ratzinger's thinking said: "This decision shows a deep rejection of Curran's distinction between fallible and infallible teaching. Ratzinger is stating that infallibility is not a category that can be collapsed simply to solemn declarations, and this raises powerful questions about how one identifies infallible teachings in the realm of moral doctrine...." Vatican officials said that, to the extent that the priest's dissent had provoked severe punishment, Cardinal Ratzinger had implicitly applied the cloak of infallibility to such positions as the prohibition on homosexual acts and artificial birth control, even though that status had never been solemnly proclaimed.[2]

---

[1] Charles E. Curran, *Faithful Dissent* (Kansas City: Sheed & Ward, 1986), p. 46.

[2] Robert Suro, *New York Times,* August 20, 1986.

Curran's dismissal has widespread implications both within the
Roman Catholic church and in its dialogue with other Christian
churches. In ecumenical dialogue, Roman teaching on infallibility has long been a stumbling block. Within the Catholic
church, Vatican reaction to Curran's dissent from what he considered noninfallible teaching raises serious questions about the
meaning of infallibility.

Infallibility

Infallibility is described as "the Church's inability to err theologically whenever it makes a definitive judgment about the
Deposit of Faith or truths necessary to defend it...."[3] In *Lumen gentium,* no. 25, Vatican Council II spoke of three ways
in which the gift of infallibility is exercised in the church: (1) a
pope teaching solemnly *ex cathedra;* (2) bishops solemnly defining in council, both usually designated as exercises of the *extraordinary* magisterium; and (3) exercise of the ordinary and
universal magisterium. Of the three, only the first, infallibility
of popes teaching *ex cathedra,* has been defined. This was done
in 1870 in the decree *Pastor aeternus* of Vatican Council I.

Although teaching on papal infallibility was defined only relatively recently, Brian Tierney has shown that it first developed
toward the end of the thirteenth century. As late as the failed attempt at reconciliation with the Greeks at the Council of Lyons
in 1274, the question was not raised; Latin theologians at the
council did not believe in papal infallibility.

The doctrine of papal infallibility developed out of a dispute
between two branches of the Franciscan order over the correct
understanding of the teaching of St. Francis on poverty. Franciscan Spirituals adopted an extreme understanding of poverty. In
the papal bull *Exiit,* Pope Nicholas III not only adopted the Spirituals' rigoristic interpretation of apostolic poverty, but taught
that Francis had been divinely inspired to teach it.

---

[3] J. Robert Dionne, *The Papacy and the Church: A Study of Praxis and Reception in Ecumenical Perspective* (New York: Philosophical Library, 1987),
p. 20. See Avery Dulles, S.J., "Infallibility: The Terminology," in Paul C. Em-
pie, T. Austin Murphy, and Joseph A. Burgess, eds., *Lutherans and Catholics
in Dialogue VI: Teaching Authority & Infallibility in the Church* (Minneapolis:
Augsburg, 1980), pp. 69–80.

To make sure that no future pope attempted to change Nicholas's teaching on poverty, Pietro Olivi, leading theologian among the Spirituals, wrote that Nicholas had been "unerring in faith and morals." Indeed, if a future pope attempted to change that teaching, he would, according to Olivi, be in heresy and thus shown not to be the true pope. So this first teaching on papal infallibility, according to Tierney, was developed to limit ability of future popes to change teachings of their predecessors.[4]

Definers of papal infallibility in 1870 had a radically different purpose: to strengthen the papacy in an embattled church. Divided by the Protestant Reformation and undermined by nationalism in those countries that had remained Catholic, the church had been criticized by the rationalists of the age of Enlightenment and assaulted by the French Revolution. In Italy the pope's rule over the papal states was threatened by the *risorgimento,* the movement for unification of all Italy into a single, national state. Moreover, within the church, liberal Catholics called for the church to work with the spirit of the age. They sought recognition of religious and civil liberties and separation of church and state.

Pope Pius IX and many bishops, who were often closely allied to contemporary autocratic governments, promoted the definition of papal infallibility to strengthen the papacy in the struggle against these "enemies." At Vatican I, the pope and supporters of infallibility got a definition, but opponents of a definition succeeded in narrowly restricting the papal power to define infallibly: not only must the pope make clear that he intends to define, but he can define only what is already contained in divine revelation or is essential to safeguard that revelation as such. Papal infallibility has been used only twice: for the definitions of the Immaculate Conception by Pius IX in 1854 and of the Assumption by Pius XII in 1950. Neither definition was needed to solve a serious problem in the church. Both definitions are serious obstacles to reunion with the separated churches.[5]

---

[4]Brian Tierney, *Origins of Papal Infallibility, 1150–1350: A Study on the Concepts of Infallibility, Sovereignty and Tradition in the Middle Ages* (Leiden: E. J. Brill, 1972), pp. 93–130.

[5]For a short history and analysis of the definition of papal infallibility, see my article "Papal Infallibility: The Remaining Agenda," *Commonweal,* vol. 102, no. 5 (May 23, 1975), pp. 141–144.

An important issue in the Curran case is his dissent from
Humanae vitae. Now it is quite clear that *Humanae vitae* is not
an *ex cathedra* definition. Msgr. Fernando Lambruschini, the
spokesman chosen to present the encyclical, said at the press
conference:

> Most of the theologians, while admitting that the magis-
> terium can define infallibly some of the aspects of natural
> law explicitly or implicitly contained in revelation, con-
> sider that this has not come to pass in the field of morals.
> Attentive reading of the encyclical *Humanae Vitae* does
> not suggest the theological note of infallibility.... It is not
> infallible....[6]

What Lambruschini said of *Humanae vitae* is equally true of
teaching on other moral issues for which Curran was disciplined.
None has been solemnly defined by pope or council. Therefore a
claim of infallibility for any of those teachings can be based only
on the infallibility of the ordinary and universal magisterium.

Infallibility and the Ordinary Magisterium

According to John F. Boyle, former president of the Canon Law
Society of America, the first official reference to the ordinary

---

[6]Fernando Lambruschini, "Statement Accompanying Encyclical *Humanae
Vitae,*" *Catholic Mind,* vol. 66, no. 1225 (September 1968), pp. 54–55. A letter to *The Tablet,* April 16, 1988, refers to *Humanae Vitae e Infallibilità* by
Ermenegildo Lio (Vatican Press, 1986). According to the letter, this 1000-page
book, which elicited "a warm, personally signed letter of commendation from
the Pope" and a favorable review in *L'Osservatore Romano* by Cardinal Luigi
Ciappi, "sustains the 'shocking' thesis that *Humanae Vitae,* article 14, in condemning contraception, abortion and direct sterilization, fulfils the conditions
laid down by Vatican I in 1870 for an infallible, *ex cathedra,* definition." I
suggest that a comparison of *Humanae vitae* with previous acknowledged *ex
cathedra* definitions will be revealing. How do they make clear the intention
to teach infallibly? The definition of the Immaculate Conception by Pius IX
reads in part: "by the authority of Our Lord Jesus Christ...and our own,
We declare, pronounce and define that the doctrine...has been revealed by
God.... Wherefore, if any should presume to think...otherwise...they...have
revolted from the unity of the Church" (*DS* 2803–04).   The definition of
the Assumption by Pius XII is similar: "by the authority of Our Lord Jesus
Christ...and by Our Own authority We pronounce, declare and define that the
dogma revealed by God.... Therefore, if anyone...deny this...he has cut himself off entirely from the divine and Catholic faith" (*DS* 3903–04). One looks
in vain for language even remotely resembling this in *Humanae vitae.*

magisterium occurred in 1863 in *Tuas libenter,* Pius IX's reaction against independent tendencies among Catholic thinkers. In mid-century, liberal Catholics began to call for change and adaptation in the church to meet the challenges of the age. In August 1863, a Catholic conference in Malines called for recognition of religious and civil liberties; a congress of theologians in Munich opposed Roman attempts to control contemporary thought through condemnations and the Index of Forbidden Books.

The theologians in Munich did acknowledge "the obligation of Catholic theologians to hold to the infallibly defined dogmas of the Church." Pius IX did not consider acceptance of defined dogmas enough. He insisted that their

> subjection... must be given in the act of divine faith to those matters which are handed down by the *ordinary magisterium of the Church scattered throughout the world* as divinely revealed and therefore held by the universal and constant consent of Catholic theologians to belong to the faith.[7]

Pius IX's teaching can be traced to the Jesuit Joseph Kleutgen, author of *Die Theologie der Vorzeit verteidigt* (The Theology of Former Times Defended, 1853–60). Kleutgen wrote: "Can they deny without falling away from Catholicism that the Church scattered throughout the world is just as infallible as the Church gathered in Council?" By "Church" Kleutgen meant "the bishops in union with their head the pope."

Kleutgen thought it heretical to deny "the sacrifice of Abraham, the swallowing of Jonas by the whale and similar things... always... treated and preached by the whole Church as historical facts and not as poetical allegories." *Tuas libenter* even proposed that to advance opinions opposed to the decisions of the Roman congregations on doctrinal matters or opposed to doctrines commonly held as true, if not heretical, would at least merit censure.[8]

Teaching on the ordinary magisterium in *Tuas libenter* entered the mainstream of Catholic teaching at Vatican Council I

---

[7] *DS* 2879.
[8] *DS* 2880.

in 1870.[9] When the phrase "ordinary magisterium" was introduced, it was so unfamiliar that eleven bishops raised questions or called for changes. As a result of these interventions, two changes were made: (1) only that teaching was to be binding that was proposed "as having been divinely revealed"; (2) the word "universal" was added to make the final text read: "ordinary and universal teaching office." The word "universal" made clear that the ordinary magisterium referred not to the pope teaching on his own, but to his teaching in union with bishops "of the whole church dispersed throughout the world."[10]

Thus, in addition to solemn definition by pope or council, Vatican I spoke of, but did not define, a third way of teaching infallibly, the method described as *ordinary and universal,* in which, without coming together in council, the pope and the bishops around the world agreed in their teaching that a doctrine "must be believed with divine and Catholic faith."[11]

Eighty years later in the encyclical letter *Humani generis,* Pius XII demanded as response to papal encyclicals what Vatican I had required for solemn conciliar and papal definitions. Pius XII specified two types of *papal* teaching to which Catholics must give their *assent* (*assensus*): (1) those involving "the supreme power of their *magisterium*," obviously referring to *ex cathedra* definitions; and (2) encyclical letters, where doctrine is "taught by the *ordinary magisterium.*"[12]

I have emphasized the word *assent* because of Vatican II's later, careful distinction between assent due to infallible teaching of pope or council and *obsequium,* due to other hierarchical teaching (*Lumen gentium,* no. 25). Assent is an act of faith in a statement as true; *obsequium* involves only a response of submission or respect. Now in *Humani generis,* Pius XII demanded an unquestioning *assent* to the papal teaching in encyclical letters and he insisted that once popes have expressed

> an opinion on a hitherto controversial matter, it is clear to
> all that this matter, according to the mind and will of the

---

[9]John P. Boyle, "The Ordinary Magisterium: Towards a History of the Concept," *Heythrop Journal* 20 (January 1979), pp. 380–398, and 21 (October 1980), pp. 14–29. Kleutgen was a consultor of the council's deputation for the faith.
[10]Mansi 51, 322.
[11]*DS* 3011.
[12]*DS* 3885.

same Pontiffs, cannot any longer be considered a question
of free discussion among theologians.[13]

Theologians, according to *Humani generis,* are to find proofs
from scripture and tradition for what has already been taught
by the pope.

Indeed, the divine Redeemer entrusted this deposit [of
faith] not to individual Christians, nor to theologians to
be interpreted authentically, but to the *magisterium* of the
Church alone.[14]

As for the laity, they seemed to be referred to only as the "individual Christians," like theologians, not entrusted with the
deposit of faith.

With papal infallibility defined at Vatican I, it was widely
presumed that councils would no longer be needed. Popes had
everything necessary to become the sole and supreme teachers in
the church. With *Humani generis,* the claims for papal teaching
reached their high-water mark. In theory and in practice, only
popes were needed to exercise the charism of infallibility.

Just before Vatican II resistance appeared at the episcopal
level. In a 1960 pastoral letter, the Dutch bishops wrote that
the definition of papal infallibility at Vatican I had resulted in
an "isolated dogma." Papal infallibility was "part of the infallibility of the world hierarchy, which in turn is supported by the
infallible faith of the whole body of the faithful." Publication
of the letter was forbidden in Italy.[15]

This narrow and isolated concept of infallibility was changed
when Vatican II introduced a new understanding of the church,
as different from the previous understanding as the Coperni-
can from the Ptolemaic theory of the motion of the heavenly
bodies. Comparing the change with the two theories of celes-
tial mechanics is apt. In the Ptolemaic system the earth was
at the universe's center with the sun, moon, planets, and stars
revolving around it. For centuries the church was thought of as

---

[13]*DS* 3885.

[14]*DS* 3886.

[15]Quoted by Karl Rahner at a press panel sponsored by the German bishops,
October 3, 1963 (*Council Daybook,* Vatican II, Sessions 1 and 2 [Washington:
National Catholic Welfare Conference, 1965], pp. 160–161).

revolving around the papacy. Or, to vary the image, the pope was at the apex of a pyramid, the source from whom all knowledge and authority descended. He was "the teaching church" (*ecclesia docens*), the recipient of special insights from the Holy Spirit. These he communicated through his vicars, the bishops and priests, to "the learning church" (*ecclesia discens*), the laity.

Vatican II

As in astronomy, so in the church a paradigm shift occurred.[16] With Vatican II a different model of the church became operative. During four years, before the eyes of the whole world, over two thousand bishops functioned as a learning and teaching assembly. They learned in dialogue with one another. They learned, not only from theologians who had been silenced under Pius XII, but also from Protestant observers and, because of the press, from feedback into the council from the church at large. Their teaching documents were hammered out democratically into acceptable compromises that could be approved by overwhelming majorities. Paul VI influenced, but did not dominate the council. On at least one notable occasion, his request that the council explicitly repeat the statements of his predecessors, Pius XI and Pius XII, on birth control was respectfully turned aside.[17]

After Vatican II the church could no longer be seen as a pyramid with the pope at the top communicating to lower levels what he received by divine guidance. Instead, the church was seen as the "People of God" among whom certain members — pope, bishops, and theologians — were called by God to special roles of ministry and leadership.

Moreover, as the late Bishop Christopher Butler observed:

> The Church's life does not flow down from the Pope through the bishops and clergy to a passive laity; it springs up from the grass-roots of the People of God, and the func-

---

[16]See T. Howland Sanks, *Authority in the Church: A Study in Changing Paradigms* (Missoula, Mont.: Scholars Press, 1974), pp. 161–173.

[17]Walter M. Abbott, S.J., *The Documents of Vatican II* (New York: Guild, 1966), p. 256, n. 172.

tion of authority is co-ordination, authentication and, in exceptional cases, control.[18]

As for infallibility, it is noteworthy that in *Lumen gentium,* no. 12, Vatican II affirmed the infallibility of the people of God as a whole before it discussed the infallibility of pope and bishops later in no. 25. In no. 12 it taught:

> The body of the faithful as a whole, anointed as they are by the Holy One (cf. 1 Jn. 2:20, 27), cannot err in matters of belief. Thanks to a supernatural sense of the faith which characterizes the People of God as a whole, it manifests this unerring quality when "from the bishops down to the last member of the laity" it shows universal agreement in matters of faith and morals.

Vatican II also spelled out the laity's proper response to the church's different modes of teaching (*Lumen gentium,* no. 25). It quietly drew the distinction between response to infallible and noninfallible teaching by its careful use of the words *assensus* and *obsequium.*

In summary, the five different modes of teaching referred to in *Lumen gentium,* no. 25, are:

A. Noninfallible:

1. Pope teaching authoritatively, but not *ex cathedra.*

2. Bishop teaching in his own diocese.

B. Infallible:

1. Pope teaching *ex cathedra.*

2. Bishops solemnly defining in council.

3. Bishops exercising the ordinary and universal magisterium.

This last mode, the only way in which it can be claimed that

---

[18]Christopher Butler, *The Theology of Vatican II,* rev. and enl. ed. (Westminster, Md.: Christian Classics, 1981), p. 67.

moral issues have been dealt with infallibly, is ascribed to the bishops

> when they are dispersed around the world, providing that
> while they maintain the bond of unity among themselves
> and with Peter's successor, and while teaching authenti-
> cally on a matter of faith and morals, they concur in a sin-
> gle viewpoint as the one which must be held conclusively
> [*tamquam definitive tenendam*].

This is the exercise of the "ordinary and universal magisterium" as spoken of at Vatican I.

Bishop Butler claimed that Vatican II, of which he was a member, carefully distinguished the responses due to infallible and noninfallible teaching. To *infallible* teaching, assent (*assensus,* or its equivalent *obsequium fidei*) is due, since only that which comes from divine revelation, guaranteed by God who cannot deceive, can be taught infallibly. To *noninfallible* teaching of pope or bishops, the response is *obsequium,* "religious submission of will and of mind." *Assensus* and *obsequium* are not synonymous. To give assent is to say "I believe," to agree that a statement is true. On the other hand, *obsequium* is a vague word that can mean compliance, respect, or deference, something quite different from *assent.*

To describe the proper response to noninfallible papal teaching, the new Code of Canon Law uses exactly the same language as Vatican II, with the same precision. Moreover, the translation of the Code approved by the American bishops renders *obsequium* as "respect." Respect, not an act of faith, is required for the ordinary papal magisterium's teaching.

Recognizing Infallible Teaching

Vatican II taught that assent is due the teaching of the *ordinary, universal* magisterium. How can we know when this magisterium is in fact being exercised and that the teaching is therefore infallible? Vatican I laid down stringent conditions for papal definitions *ex cathedra.* Conditions for the exercise of the ordinary, universal magisterium must surely be as exacting. By what criteria can we judge that teaching? Three questions help determine the criteria: *Who* can exercise this charism? *What* can they define? *How* must the teaching be presented?[19]

Who Can Exercise This Charism? "Who" refers to what is called in theological language the "subject" of the ordinary and universal magisterium. The word "subject" confuses non-technical users of the English language. In technical language it refers to one who acts (as the grammatical subject of a sentence). In this case the subject is the college of bishops, that is, all bishops around the world, in union with one another and with the head of the college, the bishop of Rome. They are teaching infallibly *only when they concur in a single viewpoint that a doctrine must be held conclusively.* It is generally agreed that this need not mean every single bishop, but must involve "moral," or virtual, unanimity.

There is, however, a caveat with regard to the *who.* Butler wrote of the possible existence of de facto unanimity, in which the bishops agreed but without adequate knowledge to reach a sound judgment. He gave as an example the probable de facto unanimity of eighteenth-century bishops on a doctrine of special creation of animal species.[20]

Four years before *Humanae vitae,* Robert Blair Kaiser asked Bishop Willem Bekkers of 's-Hertogenbosch in the Netherlands if a consensus did not exist among bishops on the birth control issue. Bekkers replied that he was not sure there had ever been a real consensus of bishops. "What may seem like a consensus may be," he said, "a mere slavish and subservient parroting of the pope's words."[21] Kaiser reports Cardinal Suenens's statement at a session of the birth control commission:

> We have heard arguments based on "what the bishops all taught for decades." Well, the bishops did defend the classical position. But it was one imposed on them by authority. The bishops received their directives, they bowed to

---

[19] Joseph A. Komonchak, "*Humanae vitae* and Its Reception: Ecclesiastical Reflections," *Theological Studies,* vol. 39, no. 2 (June 1978). For an excellent, detailed treatment see Francis A. Sullivan, S.J., *Magisterium: Teaching Authority in the Catholic Church* (New York: Paulist, 1983), chap. 6.

[20] In *Papacy and the Church,* Dionne gives several examples of such de facto unanimity, notably on religious freedom and church-state relations.

[21] Robert Blair Kaiser, *The Politics of Sex and Religion* (Kansas City: Leaven, 1985), p. 22.

them, and they tried to explain them to their congregations.[22]

In other words, simply because the bishops have spoken with one voice does not mean they have reached a genuine consensus.

What Can They Define? Theologians designate the actual subject matter on which the bishops can teach infallibly as the "object" of the ordinary and universal magisterium. Popes and bishops can exercise only the infallibility the divine Redeemer has bestowed on his church, which Vatican II makes clear is strictly limited to divine revelation:

> This infallibility with which the divine Redeemer willed His Church to be endowed in defining a doctrine of faith and morals *extends as far as extends the deposit of divine revelation,* which must be religiously guarded and faithfully expounded. (*Lumen gentium,* no. 25, my emphasis)

Therefore, *what* bishops can define when exercising the ordinary and universal magisterium is limited to the deposit of faith (the "primary object") and whatever is necessary to protect and explain it (the "secondary object").

How Must the Teaching Be Presented? Not just any presentation of doctrine suffices for bishops dispersed around the world to teach infallibly. They must teach the primary object *as divinely revealed (tamquam divinitus revelata)*; the secondary object as doctrine that *must be held as defined (tamquam definitive tenenda).* Hans Küng cited the prohibition against contraception as an example of a teaching of the ordinary magisterium presumed to belong "to the universal Catholic faith." Karl Rahner disagreed, saying that "we can speak of an absolutely binding article of faith coming from the 'ordinary' magisterium only when the doctrine is clearly taught as divinely revealed."[23] That this is no maverick teaching but a long-standing position in Catholic theology is confirmed by the Code of Canon Law,

---

[22]Ibid., p. 17
[23]K. Rahner, "Kritik an Hans Küng," *Stimmen der Zeit* 186 (1970), p. 367, cited in John Jay Hughes, "Infallible? An Inquiry Considered," *Theological Studies,* vol. 32, no. 2 (June 1971), p. 196. See Hans Küng, *Infallible? An Inquiry,* trans. Edward Quinn (Garden City, N.Y.: Doubleday, 1971), p. 57.

canon 749, 3: "No doctrine is understood to be infallibly defined unless it is clearly established as such."

The Elusiveness of Infallible Teaching

Let us return to the issue raised at the beginning of this chapter. Curran claims the right and even the duty, when the good of the laity and of the church is involved, to dissent from teachings that have not been infallibly taught. The Vatican insists that the line cannot be so clearly drawn between infallible and noninfallible teaching; that, in fact, teachings from which Curran dissents have been infallibly taught by the ordinary magisterium. This can only refer to the *ordinary and universal* teaching office of bishops dispersed around the world when "they concur in a single viewpoint as the one which must be held conclusively" (*Lumen gentium,* no. 25).

Do the official teachings on issues in Curran's case meet the criteria for infallible teaching by the ordinary and universal magisterium? I will deal with two issues on which Curran ran into difficulty with Rome: artificial contraception and divorce and remarriage.[24] On divorce and remarriage, appeal to the pope by bishops at the Synod on the Family asking for a study of the practice of the Eastern church showed clearly that on this sensitive issue, not even what Butler called "a de facto unanimity" existed. I discuss this question in detail in chapters 6 and 7 below.

But what about the issue that has affected most lives — birth control? Pope Paul VI obviously did not make an *ex cathedra* decision nor had it been defined by the bishops in council, so the teaching could be infallible only if it were taught by the ordinary and universal magisterium. We will see in subsequent chapters that strong response to the possibility of change by the bishops at Vatican II and the reaction in bishops' conferences after promulgation of *Humanae vitae* suggest anything but unanimity. The list of theologians who think that the necessary criteria have not been met for an infallible teaching of the or-

---

[24]For abortion, competent dissent from official teaching is widespread, including enough among bishops to question whether a "unanimity of a considered judgment" exists. See my article "Abortion: Catholic Pluralism and the Potential for Dialogue," *Cross Currents,* vol. 37, no. 1 (Spring 1987), pp. 76–86.

dinary and universal magisterium on birth control teaching is long and distinguished.

Historical evidence convinces Butler that the concept of the ordinary magisterium is too vague to be of practical use. He points to bishops at Vatican I who did not come to that council with necessary distinctions already developed to define papal infallibility. They had to work out the dogma in conciliar debate.

Vatican II's experience points in the same direction. Bishops learned in the conciliar process, and significant change of minds resulted from dialogue and debate. Results might have been very different had members of the curia simply polled the worldwide episcopacy on the preparatory documents they unsuccessfully tried to force through the council.

Greater assurance of the Holy Spirit's guidance exists if bishops teach together in council, rather than in isolation (see *Lumen gentium*, no. 25). To claim that bishops can teach infallibly when dispersed throughout the world, as long as "they concur in a single viewpoint," smacks of *deus ex machina.*

The infallibility of the ordinary and universal magisterium has been taught only since 1862. It has never been defined. Is it ever likely to be?

Bishop Butler suggested that Catholics could be sure that the worldwide episcopal college would not lead them fundamentally astray. But what does it mean not to be led fundamentally astray? Were people not led astray by faulty teaching on slavery? How valuable is a teaching authority that assures us of the reliability of the doctrine "that Relations in God are really identical with the Divine Nature,"[25] but for over 1400 years, not only failed to instruct Catholics on the gross immorality of slavery, but by official teaching actively supported it?[26]

The difficulty of knowing what has been infallibly taught can arise also for solemn conciliar teaching. It has generally been thought that an anathema indicated a council's intention to teach infallibly. Scholars have recently shown that some decrees of the Council of Trent with anathemas attached did not define revealed truth. Indeed, careful historical research is required to identify dogmatic definitions of past councils.[27]

---

[25]*D* 391.

[26]The official teaching on slavery will be treated in greater detail in chapter 3.

[27]Sullivan, *Magisterium*, p. 107

A problem can arise if what had seemed to be solemn, infallible conciliar decrees need to be corrected. The Council of Florence in the *Decree for the Armenians* explicitly taught that the "matter" through which the order of priesthood is conferred is the handing over (*traditio*) of chalice and paten.[28] Pius XII, in 1947, taught that the matter of the sacrament was "imposition of hands." But since an infallible conciliar teaching could not be corrected, Pius XII wrote that what might have been "lawfully arranged" in the past was not necessary in the future.[29] Pius XII could not simply correct the mistaken teaching of the Council of Florence. All he could say was that from now on it would be different.

Something is wrong when an authority can correct solemn teaching on the matter of the sacrament of orders, yet cannot find a means to solve the serious pastoral problem of broken marriages, especially, as we shall see, since no defined dogmas support the present discipline on marriage.

To summarize: there exist no solemn conciliar decrees or *ex cathedra* papal teaching on moral issues. No exercise of the ordinary and universal magisterium can be cited that meets the criteria of infallibility.

Pope John XXIII shocked a group of seminarians by saying: "I am not infallible." When that statement had had the desired effect, he explained: "The pope is only infallible when he speaks *ex cathedra.* I will never speak *ex cathedra,* therefore I am not infallible."

Rahner has written that it is not possible in the foreseeable future for the magisterium to produce new infallible definitions as was done in the past.[30] Issues on which Curran was disciplined have not been, and are not likely to be, defined. This has important implications not only in the Curran case, but even more for Catholics' right to know of the existence of options as they make conscientious decisions on moral issues.

---

[28] *DS* 1326. Medieval theologians used Aristotle's theory of hylomorphism — all physical reality is explained in terms of two principles, prime matter and substantial form — to explain sacraments. For example, in baptism, the matter was water; the form was the words, "I baptize you in the name of the Father and of the Son and of the Holy Spirit."

[29] *DS* 3859.

[30] Karl Rahner, "On the Concept of Infallibility in Catholic Theology," *Theological Investigations,* XIV (New York: Seabury, 1976), pp. 71–72.

Chapter 2

Probabilism: The Right to Know Moral Options

...the ordinary teaching office of the pope, at least in its authentic doctrinal decisions, often contains errors, even up to our own day....
— *Karl Rahner*

The pope, bishops, clergy, and faithful must all be true to conscience. But we are bound to do everything in our power to make sure that our conscience is truly informed. — *Bishops of England and Wales*

Catholics have the right to know that no church teaching on moral issues has been defined and to know the options when genuine doubt exists about the binding character of any teaching. Probabilism is a system developed in moral theology to address just such issues. An ancient adage, attributed to St. Augustine of Hippo, holds: "In faith, unity; in doubtful matters, liberty; in all things, love."[1] Probabilism is consistent with the second phrase, "in doubtful matters, liberty." Where there is genuine doubt the Christian is free. Where such a doubt exists, followers of probabilism, called "probabilists," teach that it is morally acceptable to follow the *probable opinion* of a competent minority.

The opposing system, known as "probabiliorism," and its followers, called "probabiliorists," from the Latin word for "more probable," hold that, in doubt, individuals must always follow the *more probable* opinion of a majority of theologians.

Probable and More Probable

In 1577, Bartholomew Medina, O.P., laid the foundation for the moral system of probabilism when he wrote that "if an opinion is probable,... it is permissible to adopt it, even if the opposite

---

[1] *"In fide, unitas; in dubiis, libertas; in omnibus, caritas."*

is more probable."[2] Many theologians accepted this approach, especially the Jesuits, who adopted it as their official position. In reaction, Pope Alexander VII in 1656 called upon the Dominicans to defend probabiliorism.

For two centuries, a battle in Catholic moral theology embroiled supporters of these two systems. Dominican probabiliorists stood on the side of law, traditions, church authorities, and confessors; Jesuit probabilists were concerned more for individual conscience.

The end of the conflict between probabiliorists and probabilists, and the adoption of probabilism throughout the Roman Catholic church, came largely through the influence of the great eighteenth-century moral theologian St. Alphonsus Liguori. Trained by a rigoristic probabiliorist of the Dominican order, his pastoral experience turned him toward the Jesuit probabilists. He promoted a moderate probabilism, which he called "equiprobabilism" to avoid the attacks of traditionalists. St. Alphonsus's influence increased greatly when he was declared a doctor of the church in 1871 and later made patron of confessors and moralists by Pius XII.

The teaching of St. Alphonsus qualified the use of probabilism with the obligation to avoid serious harm to others. If any action would seriously endanger the life or well-being of another person, the safer course of action must be followed. Thus, for example, war could not be justified on the ground of a probable right, nor could infanticide in the case of a retarded newborn child. In such cases the serious rights of others are involved.

Regardless of one's personal conviction in the controversy between probabilists and probabiliorists, every conscientious confessor, in the current practice of the Catholic church, must be a moderate probabilist in the sacrament of reconciliation. Häring expressed the present discipline of the church when he wrote that the confessor may not refuse absolution to a penitent who sincerely follows an opinion held by prudent and learned moralists.[3] My own careful, competent professor of moral theology in the early 1940s taught: "Gentlemen, no matter what

---

[2]John Mahoney, *The Making of Moral Theology: A Study of the Roman Catholic Tradition* (Oxford: Clarendon Press, 1987), p. 136
[3]Bernard Häring, C.SS.R, *The Law of Christ: Moral Theology for Priests and Laity*, trans. Edwin G. Kaiser, C.PP.S. (Westminster, Md.: Newman, 1961), p. 185.

your personal convictions, in the confessional you must be a probabilist."

Probabilism safeguards the individual's free exercise of conscience from rigoristic confessors. Richard McCormick wrote that probabilism supports the claims of human freedom against systems and ideologies that would unduly restrict that freedom. Moreover, it has helped moral theology by preventing premature closing of difficult moral questions.[4]

Since reputable theologians defend positions on moral issues contrary to the official teaching of the Roman magisterium, and confessors must allow their penitents to follow such probable opinions, do not Catholics have the right to know of the existence of such opinions? And if this is true, is it not immoral to attempt to conceal such knowledge from the faithful? Is it not wrong to present the official teachings, in Rahner's words, "as though there were no doubt whatever about their definitive correctness and as though further discussion about the matter by Catholic theologians would be inappropriate"?

The Birth Control Encyclical

The birth control issue illustrates the problem in an area of great practical concern to the laity. Many Catholic couples "find themselves in circumstances where at least temporarily the size of their families should not be increased" (*Gaudium et spes,* no. 51). Against their needs, Paul VI spoke with great firmness and clarity: "Each and every marriage act must remain open to the transmission of life" (*Humanae vitae,* no. 14).

In response to those who would allow the use of artificial contraception as the lesser of two evils in a conflict situation he wrote:

> It is not licit, even for the gravest reasons, to do evil so that good may follow therefrom; that is, to make into the object of a positive act of the will something which is intrinsically disorder, and hence unworthy of the human person, even when the intention is to safeguard or promote individual, family or social well-being. (*Humanae vitae,* no. 14)

---

[4]Richard A. McCormick, S.J., "Personal Conscience," *Chicago Studies,* vol. 13, no. 3 (Fall 1974), p. 248.

As we have seen, in his statement presenting *Humanae vitae* to
the press, Lambruschini said: "Attentive reading of the encyclical *Humanae Vitae* does not suggest the theological note of infallibility.... It is not infallible." Although Msgr. Lambruschini
insisted that a probable opinion could not be formed against
the teaching of the encyclical, it is nevertheless legitimate to
ask: What is the magnitude and level of competent opinion opposed to the teaching of *Humanae vitae?* Does a simple denial
that probabilism can be used close the issue?

Humanae vitae was issued against the backdrop of the condemnation of all use of artificial contraception in Pope Pius
XI's 1930 encyclical, *Casti connubii.* When at Vatican Council II, however, three cardinals and the Melkite patriarch called
for change in that earlier papal teaching, they received spontaneous applause from a majority of the assembled bishops, clear
evidence that a unanimity of opinion did not exist. Paul VI
removed the issue from the council to a "birth control commission." The commission, as we shall see in some detail below, was
carefully selected to reach a decision against change. But after
three years of thorough study, the overwhelming majority voted
in favor of change. Of fifteen cardinals and bishops who took
part in the final session of the commission, only three voted to
maintain the teaching of Pius XI. Hundreds of theologians dis-
sented. A majority of national bishops' conferences "mitigated"
the encyclical's teaching, and many of the bishops at the 1980
Synod of Bishops on the family asked that it be reconsidered.

At the very least, therefore, we can say that *some* competent
theologians, more than enough to establish a probable opinion,
have not accepted *Humanae vitae*'s rejection of all use of artificial contraception. Can Catholics, then, conclude that there is
indeed a *highly probable* opinion opposed to the pope's teaching
that they can, in conscience, legitimately follow?

"No" say those who contend that there can be no probable
opinion opposed to a clear teaching of the Roman magisterium.
Msgr. Lambruschini took this position when he presented *Humanae vitae* to the press. He admitted that "assent of theological faith is due only to the definitions properly so-called,"
but called for "loyal and full assent, interior and not only ex-
terior, to the encyclical." He insisted "that the authoritative[5]

---

[5]"Authoritative" is the correct translation for the Latin *authentice*, which

pronouncement of *Humanae vitae* prevents the forming of a probable opinion."

Similarly, the Congregation for the Doctrine of the Faith, in its 1975 ban on sterilization, denied that Catholics could use the opinion of private theologians as a "theological source" against an official teaching.[6]

But such a position can consistently be maintained only if the Roman magisterium has never made an error in its authoritative moral teaching. If such errors have been made in the past, the possibility exists that they can be made again. Then the doubt can arise that justifies the resort to probabilism.

The list of moral questions on which the authoritative teaching has changed is long. Defenders of a call for absolute obedience to all such teaching often hold that the doctrines taught were correct for their own time and circumstances, but that changed conditions and further enlightenment led to the formulation of new positions. But such a justification can hardly be applied to Pope St. Gregory the Great's condemnation of pleasure in marital intercourse, Innocent IV's teaching on witches and the use of torture in judicial interrogations, or Pius IX's condemnation of the proposition "that freedom of conscience and of worship is the proper right of each man, and that this should be proclaimed and asserted in every rightly constituted society."[7]

Slavery

Perhaps no clearer case of erroneous moral teaching can be cited than the Roman magisterium's authoritative teaching on slavery, so ably documented by John Francis Maxwell.[8] It is true

means "officially promulgated," not as in the English, something "authentic" and therefore worthy of being received as true. See Joseph A. Komonchak, "*Humanae vitae* and Its Reception: Ecclesiastical Reflections," *Theological Studies,* vol. 39, no. 2 (June 1978), p. 223, n. 8.

[6]"Vatican Upholds Ban on Sterilization," *Origins: NC Documentary Service,* vol. 6, no. 3 (June 10, 1976), p. 35.

[7]Charles E. Curran, et al., *Dissent in and for the Church: Theologians and Humanae Vitae* (New York: Sheed & Ward, 1969), pp. 73–76.

[8]John Francis Maxwell, "The Development of Catholic Doctrine Concerning Slavery," *World Justice,* vol. 11, no. 2 (December 1969), pp. 147–192, vol. 11, no. 3 (March 1970), pp. 291–324; *Slavery in the Catholic Church: The History of Catholic Teaching concerning the Moral Legitimacy of the Institution of Slavery*

that the New Testament never explicitly condemns slavery, but neither does it attempt to justify the institution. Indeed, Paul's pastoral approach in Philemon and his statement in Galatians that in Christ there is neither slave nor free helped create the atmosphere in the West that led to gradual elimination of slavery.

But Paul's apparent toleration of slavery ("Everyone should remain in the state in which he was called. Were you a slave when called? Never mind...", 1 Cor. 7:20f.) had a less fortunate sequel. As Raymond Brown has pointed out, Paul does not have much social teaching. He is basically a missionary preacher and writer whose goal is to get people to believe in Christ. Paul dealt with social issues only if they blocked his preaching. Otherwise he left them alone, even when he disapproved. He could advise slaves to remain slaves, because, with Christ coming soon, the evil social institutions of the time were relativized.[9]

But Christ did not come soon as Paul expected, and the magisterium absolutized a message that Paul intended for a radically different situation. Paul's apparent toleration of an evil institution that was to end with the imminent coming of Christ justified the magisterium's active support for slavery as an essential element in the structure of society.

Beginning with the local Council of Gangra in 362, affirmed by Pope Martin I in 650, the record is long and detailed. For example, in an attempt to enforce celibacy, the Ninth Council of Toledo in 655 decreed that the offspring of offending clerics become permanent slaves of the church. Pope Urban II in 1089 gave princes power to enslave the wives of clerics. During the Crusades, Pope Alexander III at the Third Lateran Council and Pope Innocent III at the Fourth Lateran authorized enslavement for captured Christians who had aided the Saracens. As the fifteenth- and sixteenth-century explorations began, Pope Nicholas V in 1454 granted to King Alfonso V of Portugal and his son, Prince Henry the Navigator,

---

(Chichester: Rose, 1975). Maxwell's article and his book both tell of the popes who, without changing the official teaching, worked against the institution of slavery.

[9] "Origins of the Church in the New Testament," lecture on tape at St. Paul's Priory, St. Paul, Minn.

full and free permission... to capture, conquer and subju-
gate all Saracens and pagans whatsoever and other enemies
of Christ... and to bring their persons into perpetual slavery. [This permission the pope granted] with full knowl
edge by our Apostolic power.

For centuries, theologians did not question the morality of slavery, but only debated whether the firmly established teaching
was a matter of faith (*de fide*) or merely theologically certain.

In 1839, Gregory XVI's widely cited condemnation of the
slave trade was interpreted by bishops in the southern United
States as referring only to the transatlantic slave trade and not
to domestic slavery. Many episcopal statements recommended
manumission or, at least, better treatment of slaves, but none
explicitly condemned slavery as immoral.

In fact, American bishops considered slavery a political, not
a moral issue, and carefully avoided discussing it in the episcopal councils. Even after the Civil War had begun, bishops at
the Third Provincial Council of Cincinnati in 1861 wrote: "The
spirit of the Catholic Church is eminently conservative. They
do not think it their province to enter into the political arena."[10]

As late as 1866, after slavery had been abolished in the
United States and several Latin American countries, the Holy
Office issued an instruction reaffirming the moral justification
of slavery. According to this instruction, slavery, considered in
its essential nature, is not contrary to the

natural and divine law, and there can be several just ti-
tles of slavery.... It is not contrary to the divine law for
a slave to be bought, sold, or given, provided that... due
conditions are observed.

In 1891, Leo XIII finally took a position that, while not speaking
of slavery by name, should have made it clear that slavery was
incompatible with universal and fundamental human rights. He
wrote that human labor is

personal since the active force inherent in the person cannot be the property of anyone other than the person who

---

[10]Patrick Granfield, *Ecclesial Cybernetics: A Study of Democracy in the Church*
(New York: Macmillan, 1973), pp. 62–63.

exerts it, and it was given to him in the first place by nature
for his own benefit. (*Rerum novarum*, no. 44)

Thus the erroneous doctrine so firmly held and promulgated
by the Roman magisterium for so many centuries was implicitly corrected by the Roman magisterium in 1891. So muted
was Leo XIII's correction in *Rerum novarum*, however, that the
morality of slavery was still taught down to the middle of the
present century by some of the greatest names in Roman Catholic moral theology: Lehmkuhl, Prümmer, Merkelbach, Génicot,
and Zalba. Zalba continued to justify the morality of slavery as
late as 1958, and was, as we shall see, one of the four theologians
on the "birth control commission" who voted against change in
the church's teaching on artificial contraception.

The common Catholic teaching on slavery was not officially
corrected until Vatican II in 1965 (*Lumen gentium*, nos. 27, 29)
and even then there was no hint that centuries of false teaching
and practice in the church were being corrected. Rather, the
bishops condemned the practices of others, especially the forced
labor and slavery of the totalitarian states.

If the magisterium could be wrong in its approval of an institution as immoral as slavery, could it also be wrong, for example, in its absolute prohibition of artificial contraception, sterilization, remarriage after divorce? If such a doubt exists, then
probabilism could be used in these and similar cases of conscience.

The history of moral theology provides ample reason for
modesty on the part of all who teach on moral issues. When
there is conflict between the "authoritative magisterium" and
"the opinions of private theologians that dissent from it," how
do we determine whether the private theologians are indeed
"prudent and learned" and thus credible guides in the formation of consciences? I suggest that the criteria should be those
used to judge the competence of scholars in other intellectual
disciplines: economists, sociologists, biologists, physicists, etc.
How do they rank with their peers? Are their articles and books
taken seriously? How reputable are the schools in which they
teach? In our day there is serious dissent by competent theologians from the authoritative teaching of the Roman magisterium
on several moral issues. Not only should such dissent constitute
a "theological source" for confessors; it should also be a valid

and available source for the laity in the formation of their consciences.

The system of probabilism is not a favor granted to the church by a benevolent ruler but a hard-won victory of the forces of compassion over a rigoristic authority. Catholics have a right to that "other information" for the formation of their consciences. To deny that right is immoral. The next five chapters seek to supply information for conscientious decision making.

Chapter 3

Birth Control:
The Call for Change

> The faithful are reduced to living outside the law of the Church, far from
> the sacraments, in constant anguish, unable to find a working solution
> between two contradictory imperatives, conscience and normal conjugal
> life.
>
> — *Patriarch Maximos IV Saigh at Vatican II*

Few events have had so negative an impact on the church in
the United States as *Humanae vitae,* Pope Paul VI's encyclical
that forbade all use of artificial contraception. When authors of
Catholic Schools in a Declining Church sought underlying causes
for the dramatic decline in Catholic religious belief and practice
in the American church between 1963 and 1973, they concluded
that decline could be accounted for by three attitudinal changes:
on birth control, on divorce, and on papal leadership.

For one important indicator of decline, decrease in mass attendance, 48 percent could be attributed to the birth control
issue, 26 percent to changing attitudes on divorce, and 26 percent to papal leadership.[1] Decline among Catholics cannot be
explained by general religious decline in the United States during this period, since the rate of loss of practicing members for
Protestants was not nearly as great as that for Catholics.

The effect of the encyclical on individual Catholics is harder
to measure. My own eyes had been opened in the 1977 permanent deacon class for which I had developed a course on
contemporary moral issues. Like many priests, I had been convinced that most Catholics had worked out the problem of use
of artificial contraception in conscience, and that they were no

---

[1] Andrew M. Greeley, William McCready, Kathleen McCourt, *Catholic
Schools in a Declining Church* (Kansas City: Sheed & Ward, 1976), p. 133.

longer troubled. The future deacons and their wives convinced
me that this was not so.[2]

A physician involved in ministry to engaged and young married couples, who teaches natural methods of birth regulation,
tells me that the percentage of couples using such methods is
small. Moreover, he is troubled by the number of young Catholic wives undergoing sterilization. He thinks that many who
resort to the surgical procedure have left the church under the
impression that they can no longer be members in good standing.

The problem has not been lessened by Pope John Paul II and
the Vatican's repeatedly linking the sinfulness of artificial contraception, sterilization, and abortion. John Paul said to a group
of American bishops in 1983: "Couples must be urged to avoid
any action that threatens life already conceived, that denies or
frustrates their procreative power or violates the integrity of the
marriage act."[3]

The Vatican, in the "Charter of Rights of the Family," Article
3, acknowledges the right of couples to determine spacing and
number of offspring, but specifically excludes "recourse to contraception, sterilization and abortion,"[4] as if these were issues
of equal gravity.

We had no way of measuring this issue in lives of Catholics
until our own period of sociological surveys. Was the low level
of reception of holy communion before Vatican II due, at least
in part, to the official teaching that "birth control" was always "a
mortal sin," resulting in a "de facto excommunication"? How
many couples resorted to permanent sterilization, which some
thought had put them out of the church and others saw as one
big sin for which they could seek absolution and thus solve their
problem for life?

We do know that the birth rate dropped dramatically in
modern times in northern Europe and America. For example, in Catholic Belgium it dropped from 31 per thousand in
1880 to 18.1 in 1929. Decline in marriages cannot explain the
drop; rather the number of births per marriage had dropped
from 4.49 in 1880 to 2.29 by 1936. By 1936 birth rates in

---

[2]Moreover, they were generally in agreement on the inadequacy of the Billings
method of natural family planning.

[3]*Origins: NC Documentary Service,* vol. 13, no. 18 (October 13, 1983), p. 317.

[4]Ibid., vol. 13, no. 27 (December 15, 1983), p. 462.

Belgium, France, Germany, Austria, the Netherlands, Sweden, Great Britain, Denmark, Canada, and the United States were all less than 20 per thousand.[5]

We gain further insights from current surveys. At the 1980 Synod on the Family in Rome, Archbishop John Quinn of San Francisco reported findings of a Gallup survey: 76.5 percent of U.S. Catholic women practiced birth control, 96 percent of these used methods condemned by the encyclical, and only 29 percent of clergy believed that use of artificial contraceptives was immoral.[6] The *New York Times*/CBS News poll of August 24, 1986, shows that 68 percent of American Catholics (83 percent ages eighteen to thirty-nine, 51 percent ages forty and over) favor use of artificial birth control (see p. ii above).

Many cultural changes have contributed to the present situation in society and in the church. A lower infant mortality rate and greater life expectancy have reduced the need for many children to perpetuate the family. The shift from a predominantly rural to a predominantly urban culture also radically changed the need for large families. On the farm, every extra hand helped distribute the burden of labor; in the city, each child increased demand on limited resources of food, clothing, housing, and education. Expectation of higher levels of education prolonged the period of dependency. In the Third World, improvement in health and life expectancy has led to the population explosion that seriously threatens those regions and the world's limited resources.

In 1930 the Lambeth Conference of the Anglican Church became the first Christian body to approve the possible morality of birth control. In reaction Pius XI in the encyclical letter *Casti connubii* (December 31, 1930) condemned all interventions in the procreative act. By the 1960s the time had come to re-evaluate that position. In chapter 4 we will consider the long history that led to that re-evaluation; here we will look at the immediate controversy surrounding the publication of *Humanae vitae*.

---

[5] John T. Noonan, Jr., *Contraception: A History of Its Treatment by Catholic Theologians and Canonists,* enl. ed. (Cambridge: Harvard University Press, 1986), p. 410.

[6] *Origins,* vol. 10, no. 17 (October 9, 1983), pp. 263–264.

The Birth Control Commission

In 1963 John XXIII established a commission to study the birth control question. Robert Blair Kaiser, Rome correspondent for *Time* in the 1960s and author of a book on the birth control commission, suggests that the pope was more concerned about the effect of the church's prohibition against contraception on daily lives of good Catholics than on the demographic problem of overpopulation.[7]

In December 1965, almost three years before *Humanae vitae,* Cardinal Suenens told Kaiser that he had urged a commission on Pope John (and, later, on Pope Paul) to see if the church could take an intelligent position on responsible parenthood, and at least try to reform the old idea, "the more children the better." Suenens added: "The commission couldn't stop there. It went on to consider every aspect of the problem." Archbishop Gino Cardinale, who had been an undersecretary of state and a member of John XXIII's inner circle, assured Kaiser that "John's intent wasn't only demography. He wanted to see how solid the doctrine really was."[8]

The commission at first consisted of six members, but no theologians: Stanislaus de Lestapis, a French Jesuit specializing in sociology of the family; John Marshall, a British physician and pioneer with the temperature rhythm method on the Isle of Mauritius; Clement Mertens, a Belgian Jesuit and demographer; Henri de Riedmatten, a Swiss Dominican and Vatican observer at the United Nations in Geneva; Pierre Van Rossum, a Brussels physician; and Jacques Mertens de Wilmars, an economist from Louvain.

At its first meeting in October 1963, at Louvain, after John's death, the commission concerned itself only with questions of demography.

For its second meeting in April 1964, called to study the

---

[7] Robert Blair Kaiser, *The Politics of Sex and Religion* (Kansas City: Leaven, 1985). This excellent piece of investigative reporting is my principal source for information on the birth control commission. John Marshall, a British physician and member of the commission, writes that Kaiser's book "is an authentic account of the events at the time" (*The Tablet,* vol. 242, no. 7723 [July 23, 1988)], p. 835). Kaiser's foundational work clearly documents the existence of a "probable opinion" opposed to the teaching of the authoritative papal magisterium.

[8] Ibid., pp. 38–39.

"pill," Pope Paul VI enlarged the commission to include two additional sociologists, Bernard Colombo of Venice, Italy, and Thomas K. Burch of Washington, D.C. Five theologians were also added: Joseph Fuchs, a German Jesuit, and Marcelino Zalba, a Spanish Jesuit, moral theologians at the Gregorian University in Rome; Bernard Häring, a German Redemptorist and secretary of the subcommittee of Vatican II that drafted the chapter on marriage and the family in *Gaudium et spes*, the Constitution on the Church in the Modern World, and Jan Visser, a Dutch Redemptorist and for about thirty years a consultor at the Holy Office,[9] moral theologians at the Pontifical Lateran University; and Canon Pierre de Locht from Belgium, an adviser to Suenens. The enlarged group was "instructed to give priority to the study of certain matters of morals and doctrine."[10]

Häring and de Locht had been deliberately chosen by the pope to bring diverse currents of opinion into the group. They were both well known for their belief in need for change in official teaching. However, de Riedmatten warned de Locht and Häring that the pope wanted their participation to be highly confidential.

De Locht first raised questions about the church's teaching on the meaning of marriage. At stake was the teaching, reaffirmed by the Holy Office in 1944, that the primary end of marriage was "the procreation and education of children" and the secondary end was the "mutual love of husband and wife." De Locht asked if the pope's commission wanted to challenge that.

In his report at the end of the 1963 meeting, de Riedmatten wrote that the group unanimously affirmed that love is at the heart of marriage, and a majority agreed that love of husband and wife should not be ranked among secondary ends of marriage. They agreed on very little else except that rhythm was the most desirable means of exercising responsible parenthood and that natural law was not adequate to solve the problem.

Active discussion on use of the pill in theological journals, and even in the secular press, was responsible for a hastily called meeting of the commission on June 14, 1964, with two new

---

[9]Visser was involved in the curia's censure of the Dutch Catechism.

[10]From de Riedmatten's summary of the previous history of the commission in a letter of November 27, 1964, to Mr. and Mrs. Patrick Crowley supplied to the author by Mrs. Crowley. The Crowley papers of the commission are in the archives of the University of Notre Dame.

members added, Tullo Goffi, a priest from the pope's hometown of Brescia, and Ferdinando Lambruschini, a theologian from the Lateran University in Rome. With Häring absent, the vote was nine against any contraceptive use of the pill and five in doubt, with two of the five, Van Rossum and de Locht, leaning toward approval. None thought papal approval of the pill was possible or desirable at the time. They again gave unconditional approval to rhythm.

On June 23 Paul VI told the college of cardinals that the norms of Pius XII "must be considered valid, at least until we feel obliged in conscience to change them." He then announced existence of the commission.

Council Debates

The next significant development took place on the floor of the Vatican Council. On October 29, 1964, during the third session of Vatican II, debate began on schema 13, the preliminary document that was later to become *Gaudium et spes.* At the council, basic questions were raised about the nature of marriage, questions that so far the papal birth control commission had avoided.

The *Council Daybook* reported for October 29, 1964, that the ecumenical council began discussion of the long-awaited subject of marriage and birth control, but sidestepped the question of birth control pills, since Pope Paul reserved the birth control issue to himself.[11]

Cardinal Ruffini led off the debate. He criticized the passage in the text on responsible parenthood that stated that married couples, who for serious reasons limited the number of their children, must still manifest tender love for each other. Ruffini asked how such love could be expressed, since Catholic teaching had always maintained that in such circumstances use of the act of marriage is unlawful. He cited St. Augustine, who said that if parents do not use marriage in a Christian way, they fall into debauchery and prostitution. He asked that the teaching of Pius XI and Pius XII be included in the schema.

---

[11] *Council Daybook,* Vatican II, Session 3 (Washington: National Catholic Welfare Conference, 1965), pp. 203ff.

outside the law of the Church, far from the sacraments, in constant anguish, unable to find a working solution between two contradictory imperatives, conscience and normal conjugal life.

Patriarch Maximos called attention to the demographic problem that "condemns hundreds of millions of human beings to a shameless and hopeless misery." He asked if the church's official position could not be

> revised in the light of modern science, theological as well as medical, psychological and sociological?... The purpose of marriage therefore must not be dissected into primary and secondary purposes.... Do we not have the right to ask ourselves whether certain official positions are not subordinated to obsolete conceptions and possibly to the psychosis of bachelors who are strangers to this sector of life?[14]

Maximos asked for inclusion of Christian married people, representatives of other Christian churches, and even thinkers of other religions in the search for a solution.

Cardinal Alfrink spoke of difficulties that can lead to alienation from the church and are detrimental to the "highest value of marriage, fidelity":

> Difficulties of married life are often of such a nature that in fact a difficult conflict of conscience arises between two matrimonial values, that is, between the values of procreation and that of the human and Christian education of offspring, which is possible only when conjugal love is present between the parents, a love which is normally supported and increased by carnal relations.[15]

Affirming that the church could never condone means "which are certainly *intrinsically* evil" to prevent conception, Alfrink said that an *honest doubt* existed among married couples, scientists, and theologians about complete or periodic abstinence as the only moral solutions to the problem. The church could

---

[14]Ibid., pp. 209–210.
[15]Ibid., p. 214.

Paul Emile Léger, cardinal-archbishop of Montreal, s[
after Cardinal Ruffini. He said:

> We have had a pessimistic, negative attitude toward love
> ...Love is good in itself. It makes its own demands and
> has its own laws.... We must affirm that the intimate union
> of the couple finds its legitimate end in itself, even when
> it is not directed toward procreation.[12]

Léger praised the schema's avoidance of old terminology of p[
mary and secondary purposes of marriage and its statement th[
marital fecundity must be governed by prudence and generosit[

Suenens suggested that the council's commission and the pa[
pal commission work together. He called for a broad inquiry t[
include renowned moralists, intellectuals, lay men and women
and married couples. He expressed the wish

> that the names of the members of this commission were
> well known so that they could receive the most ample in-
> formation and truly be representatives of the People of
> God.... I implore you, brothers, let us avoid another Gal-
> ileo trial. One is enough for the Church.[13]

The eighty-seven-year-old Melkite-rite Patriarch Maximos IV
Saigh of Antioch, who spoke after Suenens, brought a new di-
mension to the discussion, since he came from a branch of the
church with the tradition of a married clergy. He immediately
addressed

> a special aspect of morals: the regulation of birth.... Now,
> among the anguishing and sorrowful problems which agi-
> tate the human masses today, there emerges the problem
> of birth regulation, a problem most urgent since it is at the
> bottom of a grave crisis of the Catholic conscience. There
> is here a conflict between the official doctrine of the Church
> and the contrary practice of the vast majority of Catholic
> families. The authority of the Church is once more ques-
> tioned on a large scale. The faithful are reduced to living

---

[12]Ibid., p. 204.
[13]Ibid., pp. 208–209.

bind consciences of Catholics only with real certitude about divine law. Cardinal Alfredo Ottaviani responded that the council could not approve the freedom granted by the schema to let married couples decide how many children they should have. Auxiliary Bishop Joseph Reuss of Mainz, Germany, in the name of 145 bishops of many countries, supported Alfrink's emphasis on the distinction between merely biological sex and human sex. He asked that the text include this emphasis.

The *Council Daybook* reported that applause for some of the speeches was the most enthusiastic in three years of the council. In case there is a question about which speakers received this applause, Häring, speaking at Holy Cross Abbey, reported on speeches of Léger, Suenens, Maximos IV, and Alfrink:

> There was a great upset and the moderators were told not to allow any more talks in this direction, especially since these men had received the applause of the majority of the council. It was on one of these days I was asked by the press panel whether Ottaviani did not also receive a strong applause and I said, yes he did, only with the difference that he received a strong applause from very few hands. But [for the others] there was applause and a manifestation from many hands.

Häring referred to the reaction "of the great part of the hierarchy, the very moment when they thought they had a free expression." Four leading members of the hierarchy had addressed the crisis for married Catholics on the birth control issue and clearly called for change in the official teaching. By their applause, the majority of bishops signaled their approval. This was the bishops' last chance to voice their opinion on this critical issue until four years later when, in statements of their episcopal conferences on *Humanae vitae,* they could again express their real convictions.

Broader Consultation

The call on the council floor for a broader consultation was met by an enlargement of the commission from fifteen to fifty-five for the meeting scheduled for Rome in March 1965. Thirty-four lay men and women, nine members of the secular clergy, and twelve members of religious orders were included. There were professors from great universities, the Gregorian and the Lateran in Rome, Louvain in Belgium, Georgetown, Johns Hopkins, and Notre Dame in the U.S., the Catholic University in Chile, some from Paris, one from Oxford, and two practicing psychiatrists. John T. Noonan, Jr., from Notre Dame University, well-known for his writings on change in church teaching on usury, was made a consultant to the commission.[16]

Loyalty, however, seems to have been more important than professional credentials. Dr. John Rock from Boston, leading authority on the pill, and Mill Hill Father Arthur McCormick, important authority on demographic questions, both of whom had taken public positions that seemed to differ from traditional Catholic teaching, were not included.

Two bishops were also added to the commission at this time: Leo Binz, archbishop of Minneapolis–St. Paul, and Joseph Maria Reuss, auxiliary bishop and rector of the seminary in Mainz, West Germany. Binz had been responsible for cancellation of a television series scheduled to update American Catholics on the current situation on contraception. Reuss had publicly supported an article by Canon Louis Janssens of Louvain in favor of the pill. Appointment of Reuss indicated desire to keep some balance on the commission. Häring considered Reuss, de Locht, and himself the only theologians on the commission open to change.

Of the three married couples, two, the Potvins of Ottawa and the Rendus of Paris, ran rhythm clinics. The third couple, Patrick and Patricia Crowley of Chicago, were leaders in an international organization called the Christian Family Movement (CFM). They had used the calendar rhythm method. However, after the death of their fifth child and Mrs. Crowley's near death in 1947, she had been sterile.

In his letter to the new members de Riedmatten asked for a brief note stating "what goes on in your own field of work or of study and what would be *answers* you can see ahead." He warned them that "the Group and its shape should remain *confidential.*"

The Crowleys wondered why they were asked to keep their appointment a secret. They thought they should at least be

---

[16]Noonan's classic book on contraception would be published the same year.

able to talk to their own CFM members. They contacted Dr. André Helligers, the gynecologist from the medical school at Johns Hopkins who had also been appointed to the commission. With his help they put together a questionnaire to be sent to members of the CFM. A study would prove, they thought, not that rhythm did not work, but that it had not actually been tried. What was needed were expert rhythm advisers.[17] In their report to de Riedmatten the Crowleys said that they had "made some discreet and confidential inquiries of various members of the Christian Family Movement." One paragraph of their report read:

> The couples of whom we have inquired have demonstrated allegiance to the church and her teachings through long services in the work of the Christian Family Movement. Many of these couples have large families (six to thirteen children). Most of them have been able to educate and suitably support these children. Some have had intermittent physical and, in a few cases, psychological problems, and many indicated that they are deeply troubled by this problem. Many expressed the hope that the church will change. A very few have given up and practice some form of birth control. Most expressed dissatisfaction over the rhythm method for a variety of reasons, running from the fact that it was ineffective, hard to follow, and others had psychological and physiological objections to rhythm. None admitted lack of knowledge about rhythm but most felt it was a distraction from the proper development of married love.

The enlarged commission began its meetings in late March 1965. Their mandate was to provide the pope with means of responding with "immediate action" to unresolved problems on the birth control issue. At the first meeting, John Noonan showed how the church's teaching developed and changed in response to changing historical and cultural situations, always retaining basic respect for dignity of human life.

De Riedmatten divided the members into three major sections: one of sociologists, demographers, and economists; an-

---

[17]Kaiser, *The Politics of Sex and Religion*, p. 74

other of medical professionals; a third of theologians. The question was raised for theologians: Could the solemn teaching of Pius XI in *Casti connubii,* reaffirmed by Pius XII, be changed? Zalba insisted that because of "a practically uninterrupted tradition," those statements were infallible and not reformable. When challenged with Noonan's evidence of change, he contended that for 150 years, all bishops, in agreement with Rome, had taught many things "infallibly" on artificial contraception and direct sterilization. Perico and Visser agreed but wanted to remain open to new developments.

John C. Ford, a Jesuit theologian from the Catholic University of America, did not agree that there was a possibility of new developments. He quoted Pius XII quoting Pius XI in *Casti connubii*:

No indication or necessity can change an intrinsically immoral act into one that is moral and allowable.... This proscription is in full force now as it was before, and so will be tomorrow and forever, because it is not a mere human enactment but the expression of a natural and divine law.[18]

Delhaye, however, claimed that Pius XII had already implicitly changed the teaching of *Casti connubii* when he approved the deliberate intention to exclude procreation during marital intercourse in the rhythm method.

De Riedmatten called for a vote of theologians: Could the teaching of Pius XI and Pius XII be reformed? The vote: 12 yes, 7 no. Visser, one of the seven, said irreformable teaching could be open to explanations that did not contradict the original teaching. Of the twelve who voted that the teaching could be changed, seven contended that the changeable nature of the human data involved made it impossible to make unchangeable statements on moral issues. Natural law, unless clearly contained in revelation, is only as binding as the reasons on which it is based. Häring noted Vatican II's teaching: "infallibility extends as far as... the deposit of divine revelation" (*Lumen gentium,* no. 25).[19]

---

[18] Kaiser, *The Politics of Sex and Religion,* p. 88.

[19] Ibid., p. 89. According to John Mahoney the phrase "*fides et mores*" in the Vatican I definition of papal infallibility, usually translated as "faith and

How significant was this vote? Recall Häring's statement that among twenty-one clergymen in the enlarged commission, only three seemed to be open to change. Now among theologians present and voting, the vote was 12 to 7 for the possibility of change.

Theologians on the commission had come a long way. Fuchs had been influenced by Marshall, the British physician on the commission whose research showed that the temperature method could be used by unlettered peoples. He explained to Fuchs that he doubted that the church should promote it as the only method. "Because," as he told Fuchs, "it just doesn't work for everyone."[20]

On specific issues, the theologians could agree on only four points: parenthood should be responsible; marriage is for love; sex has a positive value; and the church should educate young people.

And they had not yet heard results of the Crowleys' survey of devout CFM couples in the United States and Canada. Some couples were shocked at the idea of consulting the laity about a teaching they had been led to believe could never be changed. Most couples, however, hoped for a new approach. Statements like those of a couple married thirteen years with six children were seriously thought-provoking for some celibate members of the commission. The husband, a scholar, wrote:

Rhythm destroys the meaning of the sex act: it turns it from a spontaneous expression of spiritual and physical love into a mere bodily sexual relief; it makes me obsessed with sex throughout the month; it seriously endangers my chastity; it has noticeable effect upon my disposition toward my wife and children; it makes necessary my complete avoidance of all affection toward my wife for three

morals," first appeared in a major church document at the Council of Trent. At Trent the word "morals" (*mores*) referred "not to matters of ordinary Christian morality but to the traditional religious practices" under attack by the Protestants. From his study of Vatican I Mahoney concludes "that the definition of papal infallibility in morals is hurried and ambiguous" (John Mahoney, *The Making of Moral Theology: A Study of the Roman Catholic Tradition* [Oxford: Clarendon Press, 1987], pp. ix–x and 120–156). See Francis A. Sullivan, S.J., *Magisterium: Teaching Authority in the Catholic Church* (New York: Paulist Press, 1983), pp. 149–152.

[20] Kaiser, *The Politics of Sex and Religion*, p. 92.

weeks at a time. I have watched a magnificent spiritual and physical union dissipate and, due to rhythm, turn into a tense and mutually damaging relationship. Rhythm seems to be immoral and deeply unnatural. It seems to me diabolical.

His wife, writing independently, reported:

My doctor advised me, recommended the basal temperature combined with the calendar method, and was constantly consulted. The psychological problems worsened, however, as we had baby after baby. We eventually had to resort to a three-week abstinence and since then we have had no pregnancy. I find myself sullen and resentful of my husband when the time for sexual relations finally arrives. I resent his necessarily guarded affection during the month and I find that I cannot respond suddenly. I find, also, that my subconscious dreams and unguarded thoughts are inevitably sexual and time consuming. All this in spite of a great intellectual and emotional companionship and a generally beautiful marriage and home life.[21]

In his formal report to the commission Patrick Crowley spoke of their shock at realizing that even the most dedicated, committed couples were deeply troubled over the problem. Hundreds of statements from the United States and Canada showed a strong consensus in favor of some change.[22]

In advance of an audience with the pope at the end of this session, de Riedmatten asked commission members for suggestions for further work. The list was long. At the audience the pope assured them that he understood why they needed more time. This was March 1965.

Gaudium et Spes

In the fall, Vatican II changed the context for any future discussion of marriage in the church. *Gaudium et spes,* no. 49, altered the teaching on marriage that, for many centuries, had been

---

[21] Ibid., p. 93.

[22] John N. Kotre, *Simple Gifts: The Lives of Pat and Patty Crowley* (Kansas City: Andrews and McMeel, 1979), p. 93.

sanctioned at the highest level. Marriage was no longer spoken of as a contract, but as a covenant of conjugal love. Coitus, so long treated as indecent, requiring extrinsic justification even within marriage, was recognized within marriage to be a noble action. Speaking of conjugal love, the bishops wrote:

> This love is uniquely expressed and perfected through the marital act. The actions within marriage by which the couple are united intimately and chastely are noble and worthy ones. Expressed in a manner which is truly human, these actions signify and promote that mutual self-giving by which spouses enrich each other with a joyful and a thankful will. (*Gaudium et spes,* no. 49)

Consciously and carefully the bishops avoided any reference in their document to the primary and secondary ends of marriage. They merely stated that within this covenant, spouses would find their vocation to transmit life and educate "those to whom it has been transmitted."

A serious effort at the very end of the council to introduce the teaching of Pius XI and Pius XII on procreation as the primary purpose of marriage was clearly rejected. The council fathers accepted the importance of transmission of life "without making the other purposes of marriage of less account."[23] Moreover, parents were not to fulfill this task fatalistically, as if they should not have control over how many children they had or how often. Rather they were to act

> with human and Christian responsibility.... They will thoughtfully take into account both their own welfare and

---

[23] *"non posthabitis ceteris matrimonii finibus"* (Walter M. Abbott, ed., *The Documents of Vatican II* [New York: America Press, 1966], p. 254, n. 168). In 1979, the Congregation for the Doctrine of the Faith, criticizing the book *Human Sexuality* published by a special committee of the Catholic Theological Society, claimed that the council had retained the traditional hierarchy of primary and secondary ends of marriage (*Origins,* vol. 9, no. 11 [August 30, 1979], p. 168). The 1983 Code of Canon Law, can. 1055, confirmed the teaching of the council. It speaks of the marriage covenant "which by its very nature is ordered to the well-being of the spouses and the procreation and upbringing of children...." Not only is there no subordination of secondary ends to primary, but "the well-being of the spouses," certainly secondary in the older tradition, is, contrary to a former consistent custom, mentioned first.

that of their children, those already born and those which
may be foreseen. For this accounting they will reckon with
both the material and spiritual conditions of the times as
well as their own state of life. Finally, they will consult
the interests of the family group, of temporal society, and
of the Church herself. The parents themselves should ultimately make this judgment in the sight of God.

(Gaudium et spes, no. 50)

"Responsible parenthood" was now officially accepted in a document overwhelmingly approved by an ecumenical council and
signed by the pope. How this goal was to be achieved was not
spelled out in the council, since the pope had appointed a commission to work on that issue. The council insisted on objective
standards for morally harmonizing conjugal love and responsible transmission of life "based on the nature of the human person and his acts," preserving "the full sense of mutual self-giving
and human procreation in the context of true love" *(Gaudium et
spes,* no. 51). Catholics were not to use methods "found blame-
worthy by the teaching authority of the Church."[24]

Dialogue and Change

For the fifth and last session, the pope added fourteen cardinals
and bishops to the birth control commission. Ottaviani was appointed commission president. Cardinal Julius Doepfner, archbishop of Munich, known to be a liberal, and Cardinal John
Heenan, archbishop of Westminster, a conservative, were named
vice-presidents. Four other cardinals were Suenens, Valerian
Gracias of Bombay, Joseph Lefebvre of Bourges, and Lawrence
Shehan of Baltimore. Bishops were Carlo Colombo, the pope's
theologian, John Dearden of Detroit, chairman of the subcommittee of Vatican II that drafted the chapter on marriage and
family in *Gaudium et spes,* Claude Dupuy of Albi, France,
Thomas Morris of Cashel, Ireland, José Rafael Pulido-Mendez
of Merida, Venezuela, Jean Baptiste Zoa of Yaoundé, Camer-
oun, and Karol Wojtyla of Krakow, Poland (future John Paul

---

[24]Did this mean that such methods might not be against the natural law and
hence were not forbidden to those outside the church?

II), who, however, did not attend any meetings.[25] They were not due to arrive until June 20.

On May 6, after four weeks of discussions, de Riedmatten put two questions to theologians for a trial vote: First, is the teaching of *Casti connubii* on contraception irreformable? Second, is contraception intrinsically evil, according to natural law, so that it can never be permitted in any case? A vote on the first question in March the year before had been 12–7 that *Casti connubii* could be reformed. Now the vote was 15–4 against the teaching of *Casti connubii* on both questions. Three theologians had changed sides.

In his report de Riedmatten noted that the commission was not evenly divided, and that only a small number, 21 percent, agreed with *Casti connubii*. He pointed out that the pope himself had picked the members. Their conclusions had been the result of a long and mature deliberation. He also pointed out that the minority admitted that they could not prove the intrinsic evil of the use of contraception. The commission as a whole would decide not to recommend any particular method. An important factor that influenced this decision was a number of surveys that led them to a negative evaluation of rhythm.

At this point, the Crowleys presented results of another, more thorough survey of 3,000 dedicated Catholic couples from eighteen countries.[26] The survey sought to determine success in practicing rhythm: how it helped regulate the size of families and helped or hurt marital relationships. Soon the Crowleys were swamped with mail, mostly from women unloading their burdens as they faithfully tried to follow the rhythm method. One wrote:

I am on the verge of a nervous breakdown with worry, and my doctor also tells me that it would be unwise to have more children. My husband suffers from colitis, which is a nervous disorder aggravated by continued worry of this immense problem.

Another wrote: "This terrible situation cannot but adversely affect the attitude between husband and wife toward each other

---

[25] Kaiser, *The Politics of Sex and Religion,* pp. 129–130.
[26] Ibid., p. 135.

and reflect on the children." And another: "My husband is away on long business trips and unfortunately his company doesn't take our calendar into consideration." Shaken by what they read, the Crowleys sent letters to the commission secretary with hope that they would be passed on to the pope.[27]

To a second questionnaire, asking, "What should the Church do?" 78 percent said, "Change." Only 42 percent said that rhythm helped regulate the size of their families. But 63 percent said that it "harmed their marriages in varying degrees because of tension, frustration, sexual strain, loss of spontaneity, arguments, irritability, discouragement, insecurity, fear of pregnancy."

Two hundred and ninety of these couples had also responded to questions in an article in *St. Anthony's Messenger* magazine, "The Church Calls for Facts." Less than 10 percent said, "Rhythm works and we have a positive reaction to it." About 25 percent said, "Rhythm works and we have a negative reaction to it." About 65 percent said, "Rhythm does not work and we have a negative reaction to it."[28]

Dr. Hellegers reported that women had greatest difficulty using rhythm during menopause. This made it least useful when it was most needed to prevent dangerous late-life pregnancy. Dr. John R. Cavanagh, psychiatrist and professor at the Catholic University in Washington, had surveyed 2,300 women, all users of rhythm. Seventy-one percent experienced their greatest sexual desire during ovulation, their most fertile period. Cavanagh concluded: "Rhythm is more psychologically harmful than other methods because it deprives a woman of the conjugal act during the time of her greatest desire." In a note to Heenan he wrote:

Abstinence as the only means of controlling conception has left Catholics immature emotionally and impoverished financially. It has left them insecure, rebellious and frustrated. Serious psychiatric disorders have arisen as a result.[29]

Delhaye then presented an official Vatican report of a worldwide

---

[27] Kotre, *Simple Gifts: The Lives of Pat and Patty Crowley*, pp. 94–97.
[28] Ibid., p. 136.
[29] Ibid., p. 137.

survey of bishops, requested by the pope. Bishops' conferences in the "developed countries" reported that birth control was the principal pastoral problem. In "undeveloped countries" a majority of Catholics practiced withdrawal, and abortions were common.

Dr. Albert Görres, physician and professor of psychology at the University of Mainz, West Germany, shared insights he had received at professional gatherings and in talks with priests and lay people. First, apparent unanimity among theologians on the birth control issue was deceptive. Scholars who had disagreed with "approved authors" had been censored or silenced. For generations the atmosphere repelled anyone who was aware of the problems from the study of moral theology. Those who did write saw their role as defense of the status quo.

Church teaching on birth control, Görres continued, had been based on natural law. When natural law was seen as no longer adequate, it was justified *ex doctrina ecclesiae,* from the teaching of the church. Teaching on sexual morality for centuries after Augustine had been subject to serious errors. These distortions were due in part to underlying, but still present and active, Manichaeism, Platonism, Stoicism, and fantastic medieval biological ideas. It was also due to a

> celibate psychosis... a state of mind arising out of the psychic situation of the cleric, one which keeps him from viewing marriage and sexuality with an unprejudiced and comprehensive mind.

Görres asked whether some moral theologians might be "emotionally handicapped... even by unconscious stirrings of resentment, envy and aggression." He questioned the appeal to "the consensus of the bishops" and asked if there had not been such a consensus at the time of Galileo.[30]

Two women members of the commission tried to educate the celibate theologians. Mrs. Crowley said: "We have heard some men, married and celibate, argue that rhythm is a way to develop love. But we have heard few women who agree." Mrs. Potvin, married seventeen years and the mother of five,

---

[30]Ibid., pp. 138–139.

explained frankly and plainly what lovemaking meant to her and her husband.

Dupuy, who arrived before other cardinals and bishops, put some questions. "What do you think has been agreed upon?" All but five asserted the need for change and that rhythm was "suitable only for the relatively few, an elite, who have a very strong Christian formation and a low sex drive."

Patrick Crowley was explicit:

I think we agreed that the sense of the faithful is for change. No arguments were presented on the other side of the status quo other than the one that Rome had spoken once and to change would undermine the magisterium. I must say I heard no other argument and I don't think this is a good argument to support an otherwise objectionable position in what we like to call the pilgrim church.

After asking that the commission create a pastoral statement, Crowley suggested: "Our report should tell how many members of this commission have changed their views during the course of these dialogues."[31]

On May 23, de Riedmatten brought in Ernest Vogt and Stanislaus Lyonnet, two of Rome's leading scripture scholars. They assured commission members that the Bible had no teaching on birth control. The Genesis story about Onan was not about withdrawal, the oldest form of birth control, but about Onan's refusal to carry out the obligation under Judaic law to maintain his brother's line.[32] Lyonnet showed that no references to sexual sin in the New Testament had anything to do with contraception.

Another vote on June 3. Was it opportune for the church to speak without delay? All said yes. Was the church in a state of doubt on the agreed teaching on the intrinsic evil of contraception? Thirty said yes, 5 no. The demographers all favored change, in view of the catastrophic problems posed by population growth in many parts of the world. In their opinion, if the church took a reasoned position on birth control, it

---

[31] Ibid., p. 143
[32] See Bruce Vawter, *On Genesis: A New Reading* (New York: Doubleday, 1977), pp. 395–396.

could bring influence to bear against massive government sterilization and abortion programs that gravely violated human dignity.

Why had cardinals and bishops been added to the commission for its final session? Was this a political maneuver to reinforce the small minority who were certain that contraception was intrinsically evil and that therefore the church's teaching could never be changed?

John Noonan attempted a "political" analysis. Here is his analysis of the episcopal appointees, before they had been involved in any discussion:[33]

For change:	Doubtful:	Against change:
Dearden	Gracias	Binz
Doepfner	Pulido-Mendez	Colombo
Dupuy	Shehan	Heenan
Reuss	Zoa	Lefebvre
Suenens		Morris
		Ottaviani

During extended discussion with input from both sides, cardinals and bishops put serious questions to the theologians. In the final episcopal vote on the question "Whether all contraception was intrinsically evil?" nine voted no. Two voted "yes"; one "yes" with a reservation. Three abstained.[34] After thorough discussion with the theologians, several episcopal minds had changed.

How this remarkable shift came about during study and dialogue of commission members can best be illustrated from accounts of two theologians, Häring and Fuchs.

At Holy Cross Abbey, Häring told how for fifteen years he had tried to convince others, and tried even harder to convince himself, without success, of the validity of the Vatican's teaching on the primary and secondary ends of marriage and rejection of birth control. The reason he could not accept Rome's position: he never published without consulting married people. He

---

[33]Ibid., p. 155.
[34]The nine were: Dearden, Doepfner, Dupuy, Lefebvre, Pulido-Mendez, Reuss, Shehan, Suenens, and Zoa. Binz, Gracias, and Heenan abstained. Colombo, Morris, and Ottaviani voted to maintain the old teaching.

tried to keep to traditional teaching, explaining it pastorally and pointing to doubts when they were evident.

His conversion came when he was called to the Holy Office several times from 1959 to 1962. He was told that he could not deny that married love was secondary in marriage. Häring, the eleventh of twelve children, said to Ottaviani:

> I repeat and I will repeat to the honor of my parents... that for them married love was not a secondary thing. That they could educate us in harmony was greatly due to the fact that for them married love was a great reality.

Gracias, aware that Fuchs had not originally held views he now expressed, asked what had happened. Fuchs explained that the theologians on the commission, who had also served as experts at the council, had "made this change, some sooner, some later." His doubts began in 1963. In the academic year 1965–66, he stopped teaching at the Gregorian University because he could not be responsible for teaching a doctrine he himself did not accept. In 1965 he forbade reprinting his textbook, *De castitate.* His understanding of natural law had changed and he saw that, since *Casti connubii,* doctrine had evolved in the teaching of Pius XII and Vatican II, an evolution away from the idea that each contraceptive act is intrinsically evil. Everyone on the commission, he said, "both from the right and the left, agreed that the pill presented no special moral case."

On June 28, 1966, Doepfner and de Riedmatten took the commission's final report to the pope. The commission agreed not to submit majority and minority reports. However, Ottaviani and Ford took it upon themselves to present their opposing position to the pope. This mistakenly became known as the "minority report" of the commission.

The Long Delay

It would be two years, one month, and a day before the pope spoke. The story of maneuvering in that period is well told in Kaiser's book. A powerful clique in the Vatican bureaucracy, under the leadership of Ottaviani, had fought bitterly at the council against change in church teaching on marriage. At the last minute they had tried to force through, without debate, four amendments to *Gaudium et spes* that would have explicitly reaffirmed the teaching of Pius XI and Pius XII on marriage and contraception. They failed. So ended the last attempt at "railroading" the council.[35]

Opponents of change had lost the battle in the council, where the section on marriage was approved by a vote of 2,047 to 155 and was signed by the pope. Now they had again lost the battle in the birth control commission. Could they persuade the pope, not only to reject the findings of his birth control commission, but to act against the clear direction of a great ecumenical council?

Häring reported at Holy Cross Abbey that, as far as he knew, the commission was not further consulted. Only that small minority that sustained *Casti connubii* was consulted. "I have evidence," he claimed, "evidence for the formation of my own conscience, [that] it was a test case for the curia to affirm that encyclicals stand higher than the council decrees."

Häring received four warnings from the curia, the first in January 1967, because he said in an interview that the pope's decision would be in accord "with the fuller development of *Gaudium et spes,* and not simply a returning to *Casti connubii.*" He was told by Archbishop Parente: "You cannot say this. The pope is totally free to return to *Casti connubii.* He is not bound by the council."

On another occasion he "was told that doctrine is not to be taken from the council since *Gaudium et spes* is only a pastoral text while *Casti connubii* is pure doctrine." Häring explained that he could not reconcile that with the opening address of John XXIII, who insisted that the genuine teaching office of the church is thoroughly pastoral. To assert that *Casti connubii* is not pastoral, only pure doctrine, asserts that it is wrong doctrine. He continued:

We had no possibility to approach the pope. In my eyes he was walled in and thus came to this document which, in my eyes, is a test case of non-collegial exercise of papal authority.

---

[35]Norman St. John-Stevens, *The Agonizing Choice: Birth Control, Religion and the Law* (London: Eyre & Spottiswoode, 1971), pp. 112–115.

Pope Paul VI's encyclical letter *Humanae vitae* was finally published on Monday morning, July 29, 1968. The long wait was finally over.

Chapter 4

Birth Control:
Old Wine in New Wineskins

The mutual molding of a husband and wife, this determined effort to perfect each other can, in a very real sense, be said to be the chief [*primaria*]
reason and purpose of matrimony, provided matrimony be looked at not
in the restricted sense as instituted for the proper conception and education of the child, but more widely as the blending of life as a whole and
the mutual interchange of sharing thereof.
— *Pius XI,* Casti connubii, *no. 24, paragraph omitted from the 1930
translation of the National Catholic Welfare Conference*

The long awaited encyclical *Humanae vitae* had arrived. With
its statement that "Each and every marriage act must remain
open to the transmission of life" (no. 14) it was immediately
clear that Paul VI had ignored significant developments in the
teaching on marriage at Vatican II and had rejected his own
birth control commission's recommendations.

Although written in the language of *Gaudium et spes, Humanae vitae* actually reaffirms certain aspects of the teachings
of Pius XI and Pius XII, which the council, despite great pres-
sure, had refused to endorse. Thus, while the language of *Humanae vitae* derives from contemporary personalist philosophy
accepted by the council, doctrinal teaching at the heart of the
encyclical comes from a particular understanding of natural law
derived ultimately from Stoicism, especially from the Roman
jurist Ulpian (d. 228). It is the old wine in new wineskins.

Why did Paul VI ignore the more humane and personalis-
tic teaching on responsible parenthood that his own birth control commission, following *Gaudium et spes,* had recommended?
Why did he return to a rigoristic teaching based on a Stoic
understanding of natural law? As Rahner wrote:

It becomes clear in the encyclical itself that the real and
primary reason for adhering to this position is the need

that is felt to hold firm to the traditional teaching of Pius
XI and Pius XII.[1]

This was the teaching that Paul VI, as Cardinal Montini, had
publicly upheld as undersecretary of state under Pius XII.
    The pope gave his own reasons: because of lack of unanimity
within the birth control commission and, he continued,

> especially because certain approaches and criteria for a so-
> lution to this question had emerged which were at variance
> with the moral doctrine on marriage constantly taught by
> the magisterium of the Church. (*Humanae vitae,* no. 6).

In paragraph 4 of *Humanae vitae,* Paul referred to the church's
"consistent teaching on the nature of marriage, on the correct
use of conjugal rights and on all the duties of husband and wife."
    What is to be said about these two reasons: lack of unanim-
ity within the birth control commission and departure from the
constant, consistent teaching of the church on marriage? Although not quite unanimous, the vote for change by the birth
control commission, which he himself had chosen, had been
overwhelming. As for the pope's need to sustain the magisterium's constant, consistent teaching, ample evidence exists of
dramatic shifts in that teaching over the centuries.
    First, we will review the history of the church's teaching on
"the correct use of conjugal rights" and the encyclical's misuse of
Gaudium et spes. This will supply the context for evaluating the
encyclical and its meaning in married Catholics' lives. Reaction
to the encyclical and the significance of that reaction will be
treated in the next chapter.

The Stoic Tradition and Clerical Power

Beginning with Justin Martyr early in the second century up to
the *Roman Catechism* in the sixteenth, the constant teaching
of Christian writers on marriage was that the use of the marriage act could be justified only by the intention to procreate.
Justin Martyr wrote in his *Apology for Christians:* "We Christians either marry only to produce children, or, if we refuse to

---

[1] "On the Encyclical 'Humanae Vitae,'" *Theological Investigations,* XI (New
York: Seabury, 1982), p. 266.

marry, are completely continent."[2] Athenagoras, in his address to the emperor in 177, explained that like a farmer who does not sow seed into his already planted field until after harvest, so Christians avoid intercourse during pregnancy, since they marry only to produce children.[3] Such was the teaching of the church Fathers.

Since no basis for such a teaching is present in the Hebrew scriptures or in Jesus' teaching, the question arises: where did it come from?

As James Brundage has pointed out, the immediate source of influence on Christian writers was the Stoics, whose high ideals for morality challenged the Christians to emulation.[4] The famous Stoic jurist Ulpian supplied to Christian writers an understanding of natural law as that which is common to human beings and animals.

Clement of Alexandria's treatment of the purposes of marriage paraphrased Musonius Rufus, influential Stoic teacher in Rome, who taught that conjugal intercourse could be morally justified only for procreation; even in marriage, intercourse for pleasure was reprehensible. For Clement, "To have coition other than to procreate children is to do injury to nature."[5] Indeed, with God's grace Christians can attain a higher ideal than pagan Stoics:

> The human ideal of continence, I mean that which is set forth by Greek philosophers, teaches that one should fight desire and not be subservient to it so as to bring it to practical effect. But our ideal is not to experience desire at all.[6]

Origen, in the next generation, taught that a man should have

---

[2] i.29, *PG* 6:373.

[3] John T. Noonan, Jr., *Contraception: A History of Its Treatment by Catholic Theologians and Canonists,* enl. ed. (Cambridge: Belknap Press of the Harvard University Press, 1986) is my principal source for the history of the changing tradition on marriage.

[4] James A. Brundage, " 'Allas! That Evere Love Was Synne': Sex and Medieval Canon Law," *Catholic Historical Review,* vol. 82, no. 1 (January 1986), pp. 1–13.

[5] *Paedagogus* 2.10.95.3, *GCS* 12:214.

[6] *Stromata* 3.7.57; *GCS* 15:222.

intercourse with his wife "only for the sake of posterity."[7] Clement, Origen, and the *Didascalia,* a collection of canons from Syria in the third century, forbade intercourse with a pregnant wife since this is not to produce children, but for pleasure.

In the fourth and fifth centuries, Stoic sexual ethics was combined with ideas about ritual purity from the Hebrew scriptures and with primitive ideas about the relationship between sex and the holy. This development established a basis for insistence on priestly abstinence from intercourse before celebrating the Eucharist, which led to a demand for clerical celibacy.[8]

There may, however, have been another reason to account for the anti-sexuality in the early church. Samuel Laeuchli suggests that the clergy used control of sexuality to dominate the laity.[9] In an in-depth analysis of the canons of the Council of Elvira (Spain, c. 309), Laeuchli calculates that, in marked contrast to treatment of sexual matters in the Bible, more than 46 percent of Elvira's eighty-one canons deal with sexual transgressions and the gravest punishments are applied to them.

The three capital sins, subject to canonical penance in the early church, were murder, apostasy, and adultery. The seriousness of murder needs no explanation. In the century before Elvira, efforts to force Christians to conform to the imperial cult had made idolatry, with its accompanying apostasy, one of the gravest threats to the church.

Now, however, as persecutions came to an end and Christianity's establishment as the empire's official religion drew near, the issue of apostasy became less important and the clergy shifted their emphasis to controlling the laity in their sexual behavior. In the decrees of the Council of Elvira only 12.4 percent dealt with idolatry.

If the bishops at Elvira imposed a rigid anti-sexual discipline on believers in general, canon 33 of Elvira represents an extraordinary attempt of celibate bishops at the synod to control the lives of their married clerical confreres. The canon decreed:

---

[7]"Third Homily on Genesis 6," *GCS* 29:47.

[8]James A. Brundage, *Law, Sex and Christian Society in Medieval Europe* (Chicago: University of Chicago Press, 1987), pp. 3, 69–70.

[9]Samuel Laeuchli, *Power and Sexuality: The Emergence of Canon Law at the Synod of Elvira* (Philadelphia: Temple University Press, 1972), p. 89.

> Bishops, presbyters, and deacons and all other clerics having a position in the ministry are ordered to abstain completely from their wives and not to have children. Whoever, in fact, does this, shall be expelled from the dignity of the clerical state.[10]

Laeuchli proposes that the celibate bishops' insistence that married clergy not have intercourse with their wives was an effort to distinguish the clergy as a purer, higher caste, superior to the laity. Use of the phrase "dignity of the clerical state" betrays a mentality of belonging to a higher order, confirmed by the presence of fifteen decrees dealing with hierarchical order. The clergy, because they lived such ascetical lives, could claim a special right to leadership in the church.

In the strongly anti-sexual atmosphere of the world in which Elvira was held, no marriage would have been the ideal. The apostle Paul had agreed, but, of course, not even he could eliminate the institution of marriage. Bishops and presbyters at Elvira, therefore, created a double standard, a superior, non-sexual way of life for the clergy, above that of the laity. The clergy determined what was permitted and what was forbidden in the laity's sexual behavior and enforced their decisions with the threat of excommunication in this life and damnation in the next.

Later in the fourth century, Jerome enthusiastically accepted Stoicism's negative understanding of marital morality.[11] He saw the marital act as lustful, unless for procreation. Jerome reworded a Stoic epigram to read: "An adulterer is he who is too ardent a lover of his wife." This saying, with others from the Stoic Seneca, became for centuries watchwords of those defending an exclusively procreative purpose for intercourse.

Augustine agreed. Only a spouse who rendered the "debt" at the other's request could lawfully have intercourse without a procreative intention. Augustine went further. He integrated Stoic teaching into his theological understanding of original sin and concupiscence. Concupiscence and original sin were not identical, but rather concupiscence resulted from original sin. It

---

[10]Ibid., p. 150.

[11]See Brundage, *Law, Sex and Christian Society in Medieval Europe*, pp. 89–93.

was the "heat" that always accompanied copulation, the "confusion of lust," "the law of sin." Evidence for concupiscence's existence was reason's inability to control the generative organs. Since original sin is transmitted by exercise of concupiscence, sexual intercourse, stained by concupiscence, could only be justified by a procreative intention. Augustine's teaching has dominated the Roman Catholic church to our day.

Powerful reinforcement for this anti-sexual morality came from one of the most important early popes, Gregory the Great (590–604). In his influential *Pastoral Rule* Gregory taught that not only was a procreative intention necessary, but that those who "mixed" any pleasure with the marital act "transgressed the law of marriage." They had "befouled" their intercourse by their "pleasures."[12] Gregory wrote St. Augustine of Canterbury that "even lawful intercourse cannot take place without fleshly desire... [which] can by no means be without sin."[13] Stoic distrust of pleasure was pushed to the limit.

This tradition was maintained for centuries, at first by the monks and bishops, writers and enforcers of the penitentials from the sixth through the eleventh centuries, then by the canonists and theologians. The twelfth-century theologian Peter Lombard stated that "coitus is reprehensible and evil, unless it be excused by the goods of marriage."[14] Only the good of offspring justified intercourse.[15]

However, in terms of the categorization of the "sin" of intercourse without procreative intent, these men were not as harsh as we might expect. Those who went beyond the intention of procreating were guilty of venial sin.[16] Gratian considered intercourse with a contraceptive intent a very slight sin like excessive talking, eating after hunger is satisfied, being annoyed at a persistent beggar, or being late for divine services because of oversleeping.[17]

A few writers began to suggest that marital sex had values apart from procreation. St. Bernard of Clairvaux considered it a

---

[12]3.7, *PL* 77:102.

[13]Betram Colgrave and R.A.B. Mynors, eds., *Bede's Ecclesiastical History of the English People* (Oxford: Clarendon Press, 1969), pp. 95–97.

[14]*Sentences* 4.26.2.

[15]Ibid., 4.31.5.

[16]Ibid., 4.31.8.

[17]Brundage, *Love, Sex and Christian Society in Medieval Europe*, p. 241.

legitimate outlet for sexual urges that might otherwise lead to debauchery, incest, or homosexual activity. According to Anselm of Laon, love in marriage had its own value: even a childless marriage had merit if the couple loved one another. Nevertheless these writers had reservations, and Hugh of St. Victor encouraged couples to subordinate sexual pleasure to the serious business of procreation.[18]

In spite of this mitigating tendency, the harsher teaching was carried to its extreme in the thirteenth century by none other than Pope Innocent III. He agreed with other theologians that seeking pleasure in intercourse could be mortally sinful, and, indeed, was always at least venially sinful. He saw no valid connection between love and intercourse. Insistence on procreation as the only justification for marriage, along with Augustine's teaching on original sin and concupiscence, were fully accepted by a papacy gaining increased control over the thought and life of the Western church.

In the same century, St. Thomas Aquinas developed a "natural law" understanding of marriage in language very congenial to *Humanae vitae*'s thinking. He spoke of an order of nature, sacred and unchangeable because it comes from God. Therefore sins contrary to nature, by violating the order of nature, do injury directly to God, nature's ordainer, even though "no other person is injured."[19] Since the biological structure and procreative purpose of coitus is part of the order of nature ordained by God, not to be altered by human intervention, intercourse only for pleasure, or without intention to procreate, would be a sin against nature. This was common teaching through the fifteenth century.

Tradition Challenged, Prohibition Maintained

Gratian had written of "the second institution of marriage," after the fall, "so that the weakness which inclines to moral baseness may be rescued by the honorableness of marriage." Alexander of Hales, in the thirteenth century, used this citation from Gratian to justify marital intercourse to avoid fornication.[20]

---

[18]Ibid., pp. 197–198.
[19]*Summa theologiae*, II–II, 154, 12, ad obj. 1.
[20]*Summa theologiae*, 3.5.2.1.3.1.

That made three lawful uses: to procreate, to render the debt, and to avoid fornication. This concession, to avoid fornication, received further approval in the sixteenth century in the *Roman Catechism,* thus abandoning Augustine's teaching that procreation was the sole moral justification for the marital act.

But, in spite of the *Roman Catechism,* controversy over this third lawful justification continued. It was finally ended in the late eighteenth century when St. Alphonsus Liguori pointed out that if Paul in 1 Corinthians 7 considered one of the purposes of marriage to be an outlet for the sexual impulse, then it must be lawful to seek intercourse in order to avoid fornication.

In the meantime, condemnation of intercourse for pleasure was also under attack. It is true that condemnation had been renewed by the Holy Office under Innocent XI in 1679, but this was done with a minimum note of censure and stated so that intercourse "for pleasure" could be defended theologically. This radical change in motives that could justify marital intercourse prepared the way for Pius XII's teaching on periodic continence and the re-evaluation of marriage at Vatican Council II.

In the sixteenth century, poverty and educational well-being of children began to be recognized as reasons that justified a wife's refusal to have intercourse. By Liguori's time, theologians recognized the morality of economic and educational reasons for not wanting more children and, therefore, for refusing the basic right to marital intercourse. Ground was prepared for Vatican II's teaching on responsible parenthood.

Changes promoted by theologians during the three hundred years from 1450 to 1750 can be summarized: A procreative intention was no longer required and intercourse not only to avoid fornication but also for pleasure was tolerated. Need to feed and educate existing offspring justified not only avoidance of intercourse by mutual consent, but refusal of the marital debt by one spouse. These changes radically undermined the centuries' old teaching that only procreation justified intercourse.

With such significant changes in the premises on which it was based, why was the church's condemnation of contraception not questioned?

Let us compare what happened to two prohibitions, both strongly maintained during the first 1500 years of church teach-

ing: prohibition against contraception and prohib
usury, that is, taking interest on loans. Both pro...
been taught by theologians and firmly upheld by the magisterium.

Both prohibitions were now challenged. The prohibition
against usury was dropped;[21] the prohibition against contraception was retained. The church's condemnation of usury had a
strong biblical basis, which condemnation of contraception did
not have. Usury is very clearly forbidden in the Hebrew scriptures and had been roundly condemned for centuries by popes
and councils. The only scriptural support for the condemnation of contraception had been based on a misunderstanding
of the story of Onan in Genesis 38:8–10. Onan was not even
mentioned by Liguori in his *Moral Theology,* and Paul VI made
no use of this passage or any other passage from scripture to
support his teaching in *Humanae vitae.*

Premises for condemnation of both usury and contraception
had by now been eroded. Why was condemnation against usury
dropped, while prohibition of contraception continued in full
vigor? I believe that the difference in treatment of the two moral
problems was due to the difference in the two constituencies
concerned about the need for change.

Churchmen up to the highest level were deeply involved
in financial transactions requiring use of credit. Ecclesiastical
organizations and individuals were involved in both borrowing
and lending. The banking system was indispensable for an increasingly centralized church. It became easy to justify financial
methods so widely used by the church itself, especially since a
basis for condemnation of usury had been seriously undermined
by the sixteenth century's commercial revolution and daring in-
novations of contemporary moral theologians. Change in teaching on usury was promoted by a relatively well-knit group of
bankers involved with the church. Notable among these were
the Fuggers, who had become the popes' bankers. Jacob Fugger
of Augsburg claimed that he was involved in the appointment
of every bishop in Germany.[22]

---

[21] John T. Noonan, Jr., *The Scholastic Analysis of Usury,* Part Two, "Criticism
and Revision of the Usury Theory, 1450–1750" (Cambridge: Harvard University Press, 1957), pp. 197–362.

[22] Jacob Strieder, *Jacob Fugger the Rich: Merchant and Banker of Augsburg,
1459–1525,* trans. Mildred Hartsough (New York: Adelphi, 1931), pp. 158–161.

In contrast to the relatively well-organized bankers, who formed a fairly cohesive lobby willing to work to eliminate laws against usury, the laity were not represented and had no influence at those institutional levels where changes in condemnation of contraception could have been brought about. Married laity, unlike bankers, were not organized to work for change. So condemnation of usury, biblically based and supported for centuries by popes and councils, was reversed, while condemnation of contraception, with no basis in revelation, remained unchanged. Manipulation of the laity by a celibate clerical caste through control of their sexual behavior had begun as early as the fourth-century Council of Elvira. It continued in full force. There was little opportunity for the development of a "probable opinion" contradicting church teaching.

Toward Vatican II

Meanwhile, the final stage in this history of change and development had been initiated in 1827 with the discovery of the ovum by Karl Ernest von Baer. With that discovery had come realization that not every act of intercourse could lead to conception. In 1853, the Penitentiary, the Roman congregation that dealt with moral issues, was asked about some married couples who acted upon medical opinion that the wife was sterile several days each month. If they had legitimate reasons for abstaining, could they be left undisturbed if they had intercourse only on sterile days? The Penitentiary replied in the affirmative.

In 1930, Pius XI removed any official doubt about the morality of intercourse during the sterile period in the encyclical letter *Casti connubii.* In this document, which seemed to be based on a complete acceptance of Augustine's teaching, the pope began to undermine centuries' old teaching at two critical points: first, that lawful intercourse requires a procreative intention and, second, that procreation and education of children is the primary end of marriage to which all other ends are subordinate.

As for need to have a procreative intention, Pius XI taught that sexual intercourse in the sterile period could be lawful. He wrote:

Nor are those considered as acting against nature who in the married state use their right in the proper manner although on account of natural reasons either of time or of certain defects, new life cannot be brought forth. For in matrimony as well as in the use of the matrimonial rights there are also secondary ends, such as mutual aid, the cultivating of mutual love, and the quieting of concupiscence which husband and wife are not forbidden to consider so long as they are subordinated to the primary end and so long as the intrinsic nature of the act is preserved.[23]

Deliberate use of the sterile period for sexual intercourse was now allowed and moral focus had shifted from intention to procreate to the biological integrity of the sex act, that is, that intercourse be performed "in the proper manner" with "the intrinsic nature of the act... preserved."

Pius XI also prepared for an important development at Vatican II, the deliberate refusal to subordinate "secondary" to "primary" ends. For at least fifteen hundred years, from Augustine to the 1917 Code of Canon Law, this subordination had been central to Catholic teaching on marriage.[24] For Augustine, writing in 419, "the propagation of children is the first and natural and legitimate end [*causa*] of marriage."[25] Thirteen years before *Casti connubii,* this subordination had been enshrined in the Code of Canon Law: "The primary end of marriage is the procreation and education of children; its secondary end is mutual help and the allaying of concupiscence."[26]

This centuries-old teaching had been challenged in the late 1920s by European philosophers and theologians who used personalist and phenomenological principles instead of a traditional Scholastic approach.[27] Now an important paragraph in *Casti connubii* opened the way for a broader understanding of the meaning and purpose of marriage. Even though Pius XI spoke of primary and secondary ends, he wrote of conjugal love, which is so important for growth of conjugal faith:

---

[23] *AAS* 22:561; 59.

[24] Theodore Mackin, S.J., *Marriage in the Catholic Church: What Is Marriage?* (New York: Paulist, 1982), pp. 26ff.

[25] *De adulterinis coniugiis,* liber 2, cap. 12.

[26] Canon 1013, 1.

[27] Heribert Doms, *The Meaning of Marriage* (New York: Sheed & Ward, 1939), pp. xxi–xxii.

This conjugal faith, however, which is most aptly called by St. Augustine "faith of chastity," blooms more freely, more beautifully and more nobly, when it is rooted in that more excellent soil, the love of husband and wife which pervades all the duties of married life and holds pride of place in Christian marriage.[28]

Then, Pius concluded that "in a very real sense" marriage's *primary* purpose could be seen to be the blending of two lives and their mutual sharing. In a paragraph mysteriously omitted in the official American translation of *Casti connubii,* he wrote:

The mutual molding of a husband and wife, this determined effort to perfect each other can, in a very real sense, be said to be the chief [*primaria*] reason and purpose of matrimony, provided matrimony be looked at not in the restricted sense as instituted for the proper conception and education of the child, but more widely as the blending of life as a whole and the mutual interchange of sharing thereof.[29]

This paragraph was still missing in the widely used 1939 Paulist edition of *The Five Great Encyclicals,* but is included in later editions. Although "chief" is a perfectly adequate translation of *"primaria,"* given technical use of the word "primary" in discussion of the ends of marriage, one wonders why a synonym was used when "primary" would also have so correctly conveyed the meaning of the original Latin.

All that was needed was recognition that marriage should be looked at from this wider viewpoint. Bishops at Vatican II adopted the broader perspective in their treatment of marriage and by deliberate omission rejected the distinction between primary and secondary ends.

The final stage of the development up to Vatican Council II came with Pius XII. In a 1951 speech to Italian midwives, Pius explicitly approved use, for serious reasons, of the sterile period for the deliberate purpose of avoiding conception. Such reasons were medical, eugenic, economic, and social. With these serious

---

[28] *AAS* 22:547–548; 23.
[29] *AAS* 22:548–549; 24.

motives, he said, "it follows that the observance of the sterile period can be licit" (*AAS* 43:845–846). Economic motives were not limited to extreme poverty, and "social reasons" seemed wide enough to include population problems. A month later, Pius emphasized his intention to authorize regulation of births:

> We have affirmed the lawfulness and at the same time the limits — in truth quite broad — of a regulation of offspring.... Science, it may be hoped, will develop for this method a sufficiently secure base.[30]

A practice whose intention was specifically contraceptive had been officially approved at the highest level in the church.

The Preconciliar Teaching of Humanae Vitae

With Pius XII, church teaching had indeed come very far from earlier condemnation of intercourse, even during pregnancy, because it was a nonprocreative use of a function destined by the Creator solely for generation of offspring. From Justin Martyr well into the nineteenth century a procreative intention or use as a remedy for concupiscence had been required to legitimate marital intercourse. Pius XI shifted the norm from intention to procreate to integrity of the physical act and he affirmed the morality of intercourse in the sterile period. Pius XII permitted intercourse with intention not to procreate, if serious reasons existed, and he used a natural law analysis to determine integrity of the act. His approval of a contraceptive intention prepared for further developments.

Vatican II accepted the norm of "responsible parenthood." It reaffirmed all the traditional values, without basing its position on integrity of each individual sexual act. Rather, the principal criteria for "harmonizing conjugal love with the responsible transmission of life" were seen to be "objective standards based upon the nature of the human person and his acts."[31]

There was no "constant, consistent" (*Humanae vitae*, no. 4) teaching from Justin to the present to which Paul VI could re-

---

[30] *AAS* 43:859.

[31] Joseph Andrew Selling, *The Reaction to Humanae Vitae: A Study in Special and Fundamental Theology* (Ann Arbor: University Microfilms International, 1979), p. 297.

turn. He returned to the natural law teaching of Pius XI modi-
fied by Pius XII. He leapfrogged back over the council's changed
teaching to the teaching that he had promoted under Pius XII.
He repeated the teaching of his immediate predecessors in the
new language of *Gaudium et spes.*

Canon Delhaye, one of the original drafters of *Gaudium et
spes* and also a member of the birth control commission, has
shown quite clearly how Pope Paul, in *Humanae vitae,* used passages from *Gaudium et spes* to reinstate preconciliar teaching.[32]
He finds seven significant references to *Gaudium et spes* in the
encyclical, all of which subvert developments achieved by the
council in its teaching on marriage.

The council bases objective norms for conjugal life and family planning "on the nature of the human person and his acts,"
that is, on the dignity of the human person. The encyclical
changes the text so that "nature" refers not to human persons
but to the institution of marriage (*Humanae vitae,* no. 10). *Humanae vitae* returned to an understanding of natural law based
on Ulpian's statement:

> Natural law is what nature has taught all animals. For
> this law is not peculiar to the human race but common
> to all animals that are born on land or sea and to birds.
> From this comes the union of man and woman that we
> call matrimony, from this the procreation and upbringing
> of children.[33]

The council rejected this biological approach. It insisted that for
Christians, the criterion for conjugal love in the marriage act is
not biological, but psychological, thus emphasizing the difference between the human and the merely animal. "The sexual
characteristics of man and the human faculty of reproduction,"
wrote the council fathers, "wonderfully exceed the disposition
of lower forms of life" (*Gaudium et spes,* no. 51).

---

[32] Philippe Delhaye, *Louvain Studies,* "A Symposium on *'Humanae Vitae'* and
the Natural Law," vol. 2, no. 3 (Spring 1969), pp. 212ff.

[33] *Digest,* 1.1.1.3, 1.1.1.4, quoted in Brian Tierney, "*Natura id est Deus:* A
Case of Juristic Pantheism?" *Journal of the History of Ideas* 24 (New York,
1963), p. 309 [Reprint in *Church Law and Constitutional Thought in the Middle
Ages,* VII (London: Variorum Reprints, 1979)].

Not to mention all Delhaye's examples, a word should be said about the use of scripture. Vatican II presented its chapter on marriage as a meeting between revelation and contemporary human ideals, hence, its copious use of Genesis and the Gospels. *Humanae vitae* by contrast is entirely dependent on a "natural law" argumentation.

Noonan rejects Delhaye's position "that the two documents are discordant" on the ground that Delhaye compares a draft version of *Gaudium et spes* with the encyclical.[34] My reading of the final document of the council approved by Pope Paul agrees with Delhaye's analysis.

A "New and Distinct" Teaching?

So, without scripture to support his principal contentions, and relying instead solely on a natural law theory derived ultimately from Stoicism, Pope Paul taught that it is "absolutely required that *any use whatever of marriage* must retain its natural potential to procreate human life" (*Humanae vitae,* no. 11, emphasis in original). He based his teaching on the *inseparability* established in the divine plan between the unitive and the procreative meanings of the sex act:

> This particular doctrine, often expounded by the Magisterium of the Church, is based on the inseparable connection, established by God, which man on his own initiative may not break, between the unitive significance and the procreative significance which are both inherent to the marriage act. (*Humanae vitae,* no. 12)

Then in paragraph 14, which Lambruschini in his presentation of *Humanae vitae* to the press called "the center, the nucleus,

---

[34]Noonan, *Contraception,* enl. ed., pp. 535–536. Noonan further supports his position that there is essential unity between the two documents with a reference to an address of Pope John Paul II, "Fruitful and Responsible Love," given in Milan in 1978 while he was still archbishop of Kracow. Father Charles G. Vella, director of the International Center for the Study of Human Life, to which the address was given, mentions in his foreword to that address that Cardinal Wojtyla had been appointed by Pope Paul to the birth control commission. He does not mention that the cardinal was the only episcopal appointee who did not attend the sessions and therefore had not taken part in the thorough discussions that led many commission members to change their minds.

the apex, the heart and the key of the encyclical,"[35] Pope Paul
spelled out specific, concrete norms that exclude all contraceptive activity. He taught that

> excluded is any action, which either before, at the moment
> of, or after sexual intercourse, is specifically intended to
> prevent procreation — whether as an end or as a means.

Nor did he permit choice of contraception as the lesser of two
evils. For

> it is never lawful, even for the gravest of reasons, to do evil
> that good may come of it — in other words, to intend pos-
> itively something which intrinsically contradicts the moral
> order, and which must therefore be judged unworthy of
> man, even though the intention is to protect or promote
> the welfare of an individual, of a family or of society in
> general. Consequently it is a serious error to think that a
> whole married life of otherwise normal relations can jus-
> tify sexual intercourse which is deliberately contraceptive
> and so intrinsically wrong. (*Humanae vitae,* no. 14)

Every positive act that is deliberately contraceptive has been
excluded, even if such acts are believed to be necessary to preserve the marriage itself or to protect the environment in which
children could be wholesomely raised. There are no loopholes.
Reluctant to overturn the explicit teaching of his recent predecessors, Paul VI placed these extreme limits on freedom of
self-determination in this area of human life.

Noonan claims that Paul VI has advanced "a new and distinct" foundation for the doctrine forbidding artificial intervention, not based on animal biology, but on symbolic meaning or
significance, rooted in biological rhythms.[36] The pope bases his
doctrine on the "inseparable connection established by God" between "the unitive significance and the procreative significance"
of the marriage act, which cannot be broken by human choice
(*Humanae vitae,* no. 12). I propose *Love and Responsibility* by

---

[35]Fernando Lambruschini, "Statement Accompanying Encyclical *Humanae
Vitae,*" *Catholic Mind,* vol. 66, no. 1225 (September 1968), p. 51.
[36]*Contraception,* p. 539.

Karol Wojtyla as the source of Pope Paul's "new" and fundamental premise on the inseparability of procreative and unitive
meanings of the marital act. Wojtyla wrote in 1960: "Love
and parenthood must not therefore be separated one from the
other. Willingness for parenthood is an indispensable condition
of love."[37] The 1960 Polish edition of *Love and Responsibility*
had a French summary, and a French translation appeared in
1965. According to Paul Johnson, Paul VI, who was fluent in
French, read it while he waited for the report of the birth control
commission.[38]

This statement about an inseparable connection between the
unitive and the procreative significances, as Theodore Mackin
points out, is not a statement of a moral principle, but is asserted as if it were an anthropologically verifiable fact. With
no documentation or verification, the pope presents it as if self-
evident.[39] But this fundamental premise for his argument cannot be found in scripture. Nor can it be verified biologically
since, unlike mammals below the level of primates, human beings do not limit coitus to the fertile period. Nor can it be
verified by a comparative study of marriage customs and sexual
practices among various races and peoples.

This claim to an absolute link between the unitive and procreative dimensions of human sexuality, whether called signifi-
cation, or meaning, or end, or purpose, seems to find its expe-
riential foundation nowhere except in early Roman Stoic perception of what happened in the animal world, the basis for
Ulpian's teaching on *ius naturale.* For Ulpian, natural law is
what the human race has in common with all animals "as it is
manifested both in the sexual relationship and in the raising of
children and whelps."

For Stoics like Seneca, and following him Clement, Ambrose,
and Jerome, what animals did was "natural." Study of sexual activity in the animal world revealed a universal pattern, the ideal

---

[37]Karol Wojtyla (John Paul II), *Love and Responsibility,* trans. H. T. Willets
(New York: Farrar, Straus, Giroux, 1981), p. 236. See Peter Hebblethwaite, *In
the Vatican* (Bethesda, Md.: Adler & Adler, 1986), p. 39.

[38]Paul Johnson, *Pope John Paul II and the Catholic Restoration* (New York: St.
Martin's Press, 1981), pp. 32–33. Wojtyla was elected pope in October 1978.
Nine months later the Congregation for the Doctrine of the Faith began the
process against Charles Curran, who had led the opposition against *Humanae
vitae* in the U.S.

[39]Letter to author. See Mackin, *Marriage in the Catholic Church,* pp. 276–277.

model, of sex uncorrupted by sin. Their analysis was derived from observation of sexual activity of domestic animals where a female accepts the male only during estrus. Since such activity was reproductive, they saw coitus as inseparably connected with procreation. These conclusions, however, were based on a narrow field of observation. Like our own experience of primates until quite recently, the Stoics had contact with apes and monkeys only in captivity, and like us, presumed that their "abnormal" sexual play was due to the corrupting effect of captivity and human contact.

The Stoics were not aware, as we now are, of the sexual behavior of higher primates in their natural habitat. Among those mammals closest to us on the evolutionary scale, sexual activity is extremely complex and is not limited to the time of the female's estrus, since it performs significant functions in bonding and creating group relationships.[40] What "nature" actually teaches is that the separability of the unitive and procreative dimensions of social activity becomes more evident the higher we go in the evolutionary scale, as consciousness and conscious decision making supersede blind instinct. Indeed, as Rahner pointed out, "'nature' itself allows us to take these two aspects apart from one another and to take either one of them as our motive for the act."[41]

Mackin's point is that the pope's major premise is an unproven hypothesis, and that from hypothetical premises one can draw only hypothetical conclusions. Mackin asks how, in matters involving such heavy burdens and grave suffering, the pope can bind consciences on the basis of reasoning only hypothetically true? Moreover, the evidence strongly suggests that the hypothesis is false.[42]

---

[40] Alison Jolly, *The Evolution of Primate Behavior,* 2nd ed. (New York: Macmillan, 1985), chap. 13, "Sex," especially p. 279 on mating during pregnancy.

[41] Karl Rahner, "On the Encyclical," p. 265.

[42] Father John Meyendorff, leading Russian Orthodox scholar and theologian, finds unacceptable the distinction between natural and artificial in contemporary Roman Catholic teaching. Speaking of periodic continence he asks: "Is continence really 'natural'? Is not any control of human functions 'artificial'? Should it, therefore, be condemned as sinful? And finally, a serious theological question: is anything 'natural' necessarily good? For even St. Paul saw that continence can lead to 'burning.'" He concludes that "it has never been the Church's practice to give moral guidance by issuing standard formulas claiming universal validity on questions which actually require a personal act of con-

Grave or Venial Sin?

How binding is the teaching of *Humanae vitae*? Joseph Selling says the encyclical makes no direct connection between contraception and sin. He contrasts *Humanae vitae* with *Casti connubii,* with its clear references to the *sinfulness* of contraceptive acts, and notes the absence of the word "sin" in critical passages of *Humanae vitae.* Moreover, *Humanae vitae* does not speak of "grave matter." He thinks this a giant step forward from *Casti connubii,* which made explicit the relation between the use of contraception and grave sin.[43]

But we must ask if this benign interpretation of *Humanae vitae* is justified. "Grave sin" is a euphemism for "deserving of eternal damnation." In *Humanae vitae,* no. 4, Pope Paul justifies the church's competence "in her Magisterium to interpret natural moral law," because "the natural law declares the will of God and its faithful observance is *necessary for men's eternal salvation"* (emphasis added). The language is more benign than that of *Casti connubii,* evidence of Pope Paul's compassion and anguish, but the moral evaluation of contraception seems to be unchanged.

No explicit statement in the encyclical suggests that contraceptive acts are only imperfections or slight faults. They seem rather to involve eternal salvation or damnation. This is confirmed by the gravity attached to all sexual sins in the 1975 *Vatican Declaration on Sexual Ethics,* approved by Pope Paul. Only premarital sex, homosexuality, and masturbation are mentioned by name. But surely adultery, artificial contraception, and other unnamed sexual sins are included in this comprehensive statement:

A person therefore sins mortally not only when his action comes from direct contempt for love of God and neighbor, but also when he consciously and freely, for whatever rea-

---

science.... The question of birth control and of its acceptable forms can only be solved by individual couples" (John Meyendorff, *Marriage: An Orthodox Perspective,* rev. ed. [Crestwood, N.Y.: St. Vladimir's Seminary Press, 1975], pp. 69–70).

[43] Joseph Andrew Selling, *The Reaction to* Humanae vitae: *A Study in Special and Fundamental Theology* (Ann Arbor: University Microfilms International, 1979), p. 314.

son, chooses something which is seriously disordered. For
in this choice . . . there is already included contempt for the
divine commandment: the person turns himself away from
God and loses charity. Now according to Christian tradition and the Church's teaching, and as right reason also
recognizes, the moral order of sexuality involves such high
values of human life that every violation of this order is
objectively sinful.[44]

In this Declaration, as in all statements on sexual matters coming from the Vatican in recent years, the tone and language are
often those of *Gaudium et spes,* but the teaching is pre-Vatican
II.

Why was this teaching so rigidly maintained? Members of
the birth control commission who insisted on the intrinsic evil of
contraception conceded that they could not prove their position.
Ultimately the real reason was to safeguard the magisterium, the
teaching of two popes as recent as Pius XI and Pius XII. Häring
was convinced that *Humanae vitae* was a test case to show that
papal encyclicals ranked higher than council decrees.

Pope Paul's implied intention is to maintain the teaching
that contraception involves mortal sin. Häring spoke to this
issue at Holy Cross Abbey:

Behind all of this, of course, is the great problem . . . stated
by Father Zalba. He cried out, and I understand it was the
real anguish of a soul of a good man: "What then with the
millions we have up to now sent to hell, if these things can
be changed?" Mrs. Crowley, this nice and gentle American
lady, responded: "Father Zalba, are you so sure that God
executed all of your orders?"

---

[44]*Origins,* vol. 5, no. 31 (January 22, 1976), p. 491.

Chapter 5

Birth Control:
A "Teaching" Not Received

> Certainly, if I am obliged to bring religion into afterdinner toasts (which indeed does not seem to be quite the thing) I shall drink, — to the Pope, if you please, — still to Conscience first, and to the Pope afterwards.
> — *John Henry Newman, "A Letter to the Duke of Norfolk"*

"Teaching is not a unilateral activity," said Bishop James Malone at the U.S. bishops' meeting in November 1986. "One is only teaching when someone is being taught. Teaching and learning are mutually conditional."[1] Teaching fails to be teaching when not accepted by those taught.

Response to *Humanae vitae*'s "teaching" was immediate and dramatic. Never in papal history had there been such negative response to a papal teaching. Karl Rahner wrote that opposition was "far greater, far swifter, far more decided and far more vocal" than had been reaction to previous doctrinal pronouncements by popes.[2]

In chapter 2, I briefly indicated the extent of dissent from *Humanae vitae*'s teaching. Over 600 theologians in the United States and twenty leading European theologians signed dissenting statements. Sixty percent of American priests did not think all artificial contraception wrong, only 29 percent were certain it was wrong, and only 13 percent were willing to refuse absolution to those practicing birth control. Almost twenty years after the encyclical, the 1986 *New York Times*/CBS News poll showed that 68 percent of all Catholics "favor use of artificial birth control."

---

[1] "The Church: Its Strengths and Its Questions," presidential address opening the November 10–14 meeting of the U.S. bishops in Washington, D.C. *Origins, NC Documentary Service,* vol. 16, no. 23 (November 20, 1986), p. 395.

[2] "On the Encyclical 'Humanae vitae,'" *Theological Investigations,* XI (New York: Seabury, 1982), p. 267.

The Bishops

More surprising than the response of theologians and laity have been the statements from national episcopal conferences. Bishops, rather than priests or even theologians, are usually designated "official teachers" and spokesmen in the church. Unlike theologians, who pick their own professions and are appointed to their positions by other academics, bishops are almost all appointed by Rome. One would therefore expect from bishops a high degree of loyalty to papal teaching. Unanimous support of *Humanae vitae* from the world's bishops would have provided strong endorsement of the encyclical. But, as Selling points out, "never before have so many bishops responded to a papal encyclical and never before have their responses been so varied, and sometimes critical."[3] To say only "sometimes" critical is a decided understatement.

When the bishops at Vatican II tried to discuss birth control, Paul VI stopped discussion in the council and reserved the decision on the issue to himself. Now, in their reactions to the encyclical, a great deal would be revealed. Although in the statements issued by episcopal conferences, the bishops almost unanimously repeated what the pope wrote in *Humanae vitae*, how they did so differed significantly from conference to conference. Some merely repeated the teaching. Others presented the teaching and explained why it is valid, authoritative, and binding in conscience. Others first acknowledged the encyclical as an authoritative statement to which respect must be given, but then developed the teaching in their own way, often introducing new ideas that clearly qualified the papal position.

Selling has classified statements from national bishops' conferences into three groups. Group A includes hierarchies that clearly accepted the encyclical; Group B clearly mitigated the encyclical's teaching; Group C seemed to him to be uncertain (see Table 1).

I believe that Selling has been too conservative in his analysis and that he has called some statements uncertain that were

---

[3] Joseph Andrew Selling, *The Reaction to* Humanae vitae: *A Study in Special and Fundamental Theology* (Ann Arbor: University Microfilms International, 1979), p. 3.

Table 1
Bishops' Statements on *Humanae vitae*

From Selling, *Reaction to* Humanae vitae, Appendix B3. The numbers after some conferences refer to a particular statement when a conference issued more than one statement.

Group A Clear Acceptance	Group B Clear Mitigation	Group C Uncertain
Interim Statements:		
Spain (1) Vietnam	Netherlands (1)	U.S.A. (1)

Statements issued during the first year after promulgation:

Group A	Group B	Group C
Australia (1)	Austria	Brazil
Ceylon	Belgium	Czechoslovakia
Colombia	Canada	East Germany
Dahomey	CELAM*	England/Wales
Ireland (1, 2)	France	India
Korea	Indonesia (1, 2)	Indonesia (3)
Malta (1)	Netherlands (2)	Italy
Mexico (1, 2)	Scandinavia	Japan
New Zealand	Switzerland	U.S.A. (2)
Philippines	West Germany	
Poland (1, 2)		
Portugal		
Puerto Rico		
Rhodesia		
Scotland		
Senegal		
Spain (2)		
Yugoslavia (1)		

Later Statements:

Group A	Group B	Group C
Yugoslavia (2)	Indonesia (4)	Australia (2)
Ireland (3)	Malta (2)	
	Mexico (3)	
	South Africa	

*Conferencia episcopal latinoamericana

written ambiguously to obscure the fact of mitigation. American statements illustrate the point.

A preliminary statement issued by the National Conference of Catholic Bishops spoke of the pope's unique role in the church and asked "our priests and people to receive with sincerity what he has taught, to study it carefully, and to form their consciences in its light." Many interpreted this to mean that they were still free to decide in conscience how they could act. Then the conference's general secretary issued a "clarificatory" statement that the bishops had not diverged from the pope's teaching. People had to form their consciences, but they had to form a *correct* conscience.[4]

Selling thinks that the American bishops' final statement, *Human Life in Our Day*, confirms the general secretary's "clarification" that they in no way diverged from papal teaching. A careful reading, however, shows that mitigation of papal teaching in the document of the American bishops was quite definite.[5]

First, after serious discussion the bishops changed the pope's language from "intrinsically wrong" (*ideoque intrinsece inhonestum*[6]) to "objective moral disorder," or "objective evil." So important is the word "intrinsic" in the natural law tradition used by the pope, that change from "intrinsic" to "objective" is significant. For the pope, contraception is "intrinsically wrong" because it frustrates "the design established by the Creator" and "contradicts the will of the Author of life" (*Humanae vitae,* no. 13). It could not be justified "even for the gravest reasons" (*Humanae vitae,* no. 14).

Then, the encyclical gives no hint of a possible contrary decision in conscience. Many American bishops wanted to introduce the classic objective-subjective distinction, not used in *Humanae vitae.* Artificial birth control could be seen to be an "objective" or "premoral" evil. Subjectively, guilt could vary

---

[4]For the statements from the bishops' conferences, see John Horgan, ed., *Humanae vitae and the Bishops: The Encyclical and the Statements of the National Hierarchies* (Shannon, Ireland: Irish University Press, 1972).

[5]*Human Life in Our Day*, a collective pastoral letter of the American hierarchy, issued on November 15, 1968, at their annual meeting in Washington, D.C. For the conflicting interpretations at the time, see Patrick Granfield, *Ecclesial Cybernetics: A Study of Democracy in the Church* (New York: Macmillan, 1973), pp. 80–82.

[6]*AAS* 60:491.

from zero to 100 percent. Objective evil would only involve subjective guilt for someone acting against conscience. Here conscience, not mentioned by the pope, becomes the supreme guide.

The bishops included two statements about conscience in their November 1968 letter. While they emphasized the importance of conformity of conscience to the church's interpretation of divine law, they recognized the possibility that Catholics might, in conscience, have to reject noninfallible papal teaching. They quoted Newman's description of circumstances in which conscience could oppose the supreme, though not infallible, authority of the pope. Newman wrote that for conscience to be "a sacred and sovereign monitor," it could prevail against the voice of the pope only after serious thought, prayer, and use of all available means to arrive at a right judgment.

Moreover, when writing on conscientious objection, the bishops stated their own conviction about conscience quite clearly and succinctly. They described themselves "as witnesses to a spiritual tradition which accepts enlightened conscience, even when honestly mistaken, as the arbiter of moral decision...."[7] Not "correct conscience" as in the earlier clarifying statement, but here changed to "enlightened conscience, even when honestly mistaken." Mitigation is subtle, but unmistakable.

English and Welsh bishops, among those listed uncertain by Selling, also stressed conscience's role. In a context emphasizing the importance of listening to "the guidance of the Church," they stressed the primacy of conscience. Since the encyclical contained no sweeping condemnations and "no threat of damnation," the bishops seemed to think that it did not consider contraceptive acts gravely sinful.

The Swiss bishops reveal interesting contrasts in their episcopal statements. In an early individual statement, Bishop Adam of Sion said that one who did not accept the teaching was no longer a Catholic. He suggested that those who refused to obey the pope "should have the loyalty and courage to leave the Church."[8] Later, Bishop Adam claimed no intention to exclude anyone from the church; he only meant to remind Catholics of consequences of rebelling against papal authority.

---

[7] *Human Life in Our Day*, p. 43.
[8] Selling, *The Reaction to* Humanae vitae, p. 13.

When Swiss bishops finally issued their joint statement on December 11, 1968, they taught that those who could not accept the encyclical's teaching in their lives, who were not acting from selfish motives but were sincerely trying to obey God's will more perfectly, should not consider themselves guilty. They asked those whose difficulties were more intellectual to keep an open mind and be prepared to review their statements about the encyclical's doctrine.

Ways in which bishops' conferences expected papal teaching to be accepted differed significantly.[9] Those who fully accepted the encyclical considered the issue closed, its teaching to be followed as set forth. However, conferences classified under "clear mitigation" were only "concerned that the pope receive reverent and respectful attention." Many characterized *Humanae vitae* as an opportunity for dialogue, and some suggested the possibility that teaching on contraception might change.

All bishops in Group B (clear mitigation), plus more than half classified as "uncertain," considered the ban on contraception an open question when applied to individual cases. They introduced mitigating ideas: the conflict of duties, the lesser of two evils, and the influence of motivation, ideas incompatible with the encyclical's clear teaching. Some suggested that, rather than a strict prohibition, a high ideal was proposed for married couples. Thus the Italian bishops wrote of " . . . this norm, which is at once humble and sublime, an ideal goal to which they are pledged by their dignity and conjugal vocation." With some hesitation about doubtful cases, Selling concluded that the clearly affirming group, to which he added Brazil, England/Wales, Italy, and the United States, made up slightly over half the conferences.

A Democratic Scenario

I propose a different analysis of Selling's table. I have already questioned his conclusion that the American statement is uncertain. I consider it sufficiently mitigating to include it in Group

---

[9]"Although a very few episcopal statements . . . leave either no, or very little room for individual conscience to dissent from the encyclical, by far the larger number consider the possibility in all seriousness" (John Mahoney, *The Making of Moral Theology: A Study of the Roman Catholic Tradition* [Oxford: Clarendon Press, 1987], p. 291, n. 87).

Table 2
Selling's Groups Adjusted for Number of Ordinaries

Group A Clear Acceptance		Group B Clear Mitigation		Group C Uncertain	
Ceylon	5	Austria	9	Australia	26
Dahomey	6	Belgium	8	Czechoslovakia	12
Ireland	26	Canada	67	East Germany	7
Korea	13	CELAM	442	England/Wales	20
New Zealand	4	France	90	India	77
Philippines	47	Indonesia	31	Italy	270
Poland	26	Malta	2	Japan	16
Portugal	17	Netherlands	7		
Puerto Rico	4	Scandinavia	4		
Rhodesia	4	South Africa	20		
Scotland	7	Switzerland	6		
Senegal	5	U.S.A.	159		
Spain	63	West Germany	21		
Vietnam	12				
Yugoslavia	23				
Totals	262		866		428
	17%		56%		28%

B. Then, is it statistically sound to give the same weight to New Zealand, with four dioceses, and CELAM, an umbrella organization in Latin America that includes twenty-two national conferences with 442 dioceses?

What would have happened if Paul VI, aware of the gravity of his decision, had called a special session of the adjourned council, inviting all diocesan ordinaries back to Rome to share his burden? With the above qualifications in mind, I propose to reconstruct Selling's table, using the 1970 *Annuarium Statisticum Ecclesiae* listing of dioceses from the Vatican Secretariat of State (see Table 2).[10] This will give a rough approximation of how ordinaries, that is, presiding bishops of those dioceses, might have voted had Paul VI given them a chance to respond to *Humanae vitae*.

In our hypothetical special session, only 17 percent would have strongly supported *Humanae vitae* ("clear acceptance").

---

[10] *Annuarium Statisticum Ecclesiae*, 1970 (Vatican Press, 1973), pp. 141–146.

Fifty-six percent clearly mitigated the teaching, and 28 percent ("uncertain") would apparently have been unreliable supporters. This is scarcely the moral unanimity required for infallible teaching of the ordinary and universal magisterium.

At the 1980 Synod on the Family, Cardinal Felici claimed that bishops of the West had been responsible for reservations expressed against *Humanae vitae.*[11] The tables show, however, this was not the case.

If the pope had worked with the worldwide episcopacy, beginning with participation by bishops at the council, the tragedy of *Humanae vitae* would not have occurred. *Humanae vitae* was a non-collegial exercise in a matter where the broadest collegiality and extreme sensitivity to the *sensus fidelium* (sense of the faithful) were essential for the edification of the church.

The preamble to the definition of papal infallibility in *Pastor aeternus* from Vatican I describes the consultative process that is integral to the magisterium:

> according to the exigencies of time and circumstances, sometimes assembling ecumenical councils, or asking for *the mind of the church* scattered throughout the world, sometimes by particular synods, sometimes using other helps which divine providence supplied.... (emphasis added)

If it is critically important that a pope, before he solemnly defines a teaching, find out "the mind of the church," would not similar caution be advisable in his more ordinary teaching in a matter like birth control, which seriously affects millions of Catholics' lives? To ask how the world's bishops might have responded had they been given an open, collegial opportunity to react to *Humanae vitae* is far from absurd and un-Catholic.

Sense of the Faithful

What about the laity, who together with the hierarchy, were called by Vatican II "the people of God" (*Lumen gentium,*

[11]Jan Grootaers and Joseph A. Selling, *The 1980 Synod of Bishops "On the Role of the Family": Exposition of the Event and an Analysis of Its Texts*, Bibliotheca Ephemeridum Theologicarum Lovaniensium (Leuven: Leuven University Press, 1983), p. 96.

chap. 2)? Especially since Newman's pathbreaking *On Consulting the Faithful in Matters of Doctrine*,[12] Vatican I's phrase in *Pastor aeternus*, "the mind of the church," surely includes the ancient idea of *sensus fidelium*, sense of the faithful. Indeed, some bishops' conferences wrote their mitigating statements on *Humanae vitae* after direct consultation with laity. There can be little doubt that all were indirectly influenced by their people's faith experience. In our day, cannot carefully taken and carefully evaluated sociological surveys be a tool for determining that "mind of the faithful"?

Rahner has called attention to the dilemma of the average Christian or theologian if asked to accept teachings whose basis in revelation is not apparent, or which may even seem to be a new revelation. Paul VI's call for obedience, not for reasons given but because of special enlightenment associated with his office, creates this situation. He wrote:

> For, as you know, the Pastors of the Church enjoy a special light of the Holy Spirit in teaching the truth. And this, rather than the arguments they put forward, is why you are bound to such obedience. (*Humanae vitae*, no. 28)

The pope supported his appeal to the light of the Holy Spirit with a reference to *Lumen gentium*, no. 25. The passage from *Lumen gentium*, however, asserts that the Holy Spirit's light is given to teach only what is in revelation. Both *Pastor aeternus* and *Lumen gentium* make clear that the infallibility of the church, which the pope exercises when defining solemnly, is limited in scope to the deposit of faith. The encyclical makes clear that it is based, not on divine revelation, but on natural law. A demonstration based on natural law can convince only by the cogency of its arguments. *Humanae vitae*'s failure to convince theologians and devout, thinking Catholics comes precisely from the weakness of its intellectual foundation. For Rahner the right approach calls for acceptance of teaching because of its truth, with minimal emphasis on the office's authority.

A strange development, since promulgation of *Humanae vitae*, has been the insistent appeal to theologians to explain the

---

[12] John Henry Newman, *On Consulting the Faithful in Matters of Doctrine*, ed. John Coulson (New York: Sheed & Ward, 1961).

doctrine more clearly, to make it more acceptable not only to Catholics, but indeed, to all people of good will. In *Familiaris consortio*, John Paul II issued a pressing invitation to theologians

> to collaborate with the hierarchical magisterium and to commit themselves to the task of illustrating ever more clearly the biblical foundations, the ethical grounds and the personalist reasons behind this doctrine,... to render the teaching of the encyclical on this fundamental question truly accessible to all people of good will, fostering a daily more enlightened and profound understanding of it.[13]

But surely one major problem with the encyclical from the beginning has been its failure to convince a major part of the theological community. How are theologians to explain more clearly a doctrine about which they themselves are not convinced? One is reminded of Fuchs's testimony on the birth control commission. He had stopped teaching at the Gregorian University in the academic year 1965–1966 and prevented the reprinting of his textbook *De castitate* because he could not responsibly teach a doctrine he himself could not accept.

Even more serious for priests and parishioners is insistence on frequent reception of the sacraments, especially penance, for those who fail to live up to demands of the pope's teaching. This insistence derives from *Humanae vitae*. Paul VI wrote:

> If, however, sin still exercises its hold over them, they are not to lose heart. Rather must they, humble and persevering, have recourse to the mercy of God, bestowed in the sacrament of penance. (*Humanae vitae*, no. 25)

This advice raises a serious problem for a priest with confessional and counseling experience. In a typical situation a couple has decided in conscience that they must not have any more children. Periodic continence either does not work, or, like total abstinence, is destructive of their marital relationship. Often

---

[13]*Origins*, vol. 11, nos. 28–29 (December 24, 1981), p. 447.

with professional medical advice they are using artificial contraception and expect to do so as long as the wife is fertile. They have been taught that, unless they have a firm "purpose of amendment," their sacramental encounter is invalid, even sacrilegious.

The confessor is urged to treat this penitent as a "habitual sinner" in need of time to convert, or as one with a sincere but incorrect conscience. In either case, penitents are told to continue to receive the sacraments — "to overcome the hold that sin has on them." A penitent who has a sincere commitment to continue use of contraception finds this a recommendation for hypocrisy.

In his 1968 talk at Holy Cross Abbey, Häring said those in doubt had to study the encyclical thoroughly and with good will, but be open to other information in the church. If in sincere conscience they decide that for them the use of artificial contraception is right, they must follow their conscience. Rahner, after describing a similar process of study and discernment, reached the same conclusion. Here, however, the question must be frankly asked: how many of the laity can be expected to make this kind of thorough study of the encyclical?

At the 1980 Synod on the Family, reaction to the encyclical was complex. Bishops from developing countries of the southern hemisphere were worried about government attempts (their own and those of the North) to solve their very serious economic problems by reducing populations, without promotion of other means of alleviating human misery and poverty.

Many bishops from developed countries of the North expressed widespread concern over a gulf between *Humanae vitae*'s teaching and actual pastoral practice. We have already seen Quinn's report on the United States. Consultation with 60,000 Catholics convinced the French episcopal conference that "techniques of [ovulation] observation" are not practical for a large number of the laity. Bishop Jullien of Beauvais called upon the synod to make it possible for faithful couples to live without anxiety because of rigid church teaching.[14] Bishops emphasized that opposition came from committed Catholics, including the-

---

[14]Francis X. Murphy, C.SS.R., "Of Sex and the Catholic Church," *Atlantic Monthly,* vol. 247, no. 2 (February 1981), p. 51.

ologians and spiritual leaders, people undoubtedly dedicated to the church.

Cardinal Hume of England made a strong case for the synod to give serious attention to the experience of married laity. He asserted that experience and understanding of the sacrament of matrimony by husbands and wives constituted an authentic theological source (*fons theologiae*) that pastors and the whole church should draw upon. Married couples had a twofold title to authority in matters concerning marriage: they are the sacrament's ministers and only they have experienced its effects. Cardinal Enrique y Tarancon, archbishop of Madrid, said that repeating old formulations was not enough. The church must be open to new theological research, to the human sciences, and listen to married couples whose experience of faith bishops do not have. (In 1968 Spanish bishops had accepted *Humanae vitae*.)

Was It Received?

Bishops, theologians, laity! Doctrine central to *Humanae vitae* has not been received by a large part of the church. How is this theologically significant? What does it mean that doctrine is received? What is reception? According to Yves Congar, reception is not concerned with the legality of teaching, but with its content and its meaningfulness in the church's life. Reception does not make teaching valid, but attests that this dogma, law, or ethical rule is for the church's good. Non-reception does not mean that the doctrine is false, only that it "does not call forth any living power and therefore does not contribute to edification." Congar gives contemporary examples of non-reception and then asks of *Humanae vitae:* "Is this 'non-reception,' or 'disobedience,' or what? The facts are there."[15] Rahner proposes that the magisterium must wait to see if its teaching has been *received.* If teaching is received, the church has recognized in it its already existing faith; in case of non-reception, it has not.[16]

Can Rome reverse the dissent in the episcopacy by carefully weeding out all contrary thinking through future episcopal ap-

---

[15]Yves M. Congar, "Reception as an Ecclesiastical Reality," trans. John Griffiths, in Concilium 77 (New York: Herder and Herder, 1972), pp. 57–66.

[16]Karl Rahner, "Magisterium and Theology," *Theological Investigations,* XVIII (New York: Crossroad, 1983), p. 61.

pointments? Under Paul VI, Archbishop Jadot was told to appoint pastoral bishops. John Paul II seems to be more concerned with uniformity and fidelity to Rome. During their *ad limina* visits in September 1983, he told American bishops to seek "priests who have already proven themselves as teachers of the faith as it is proclaimed by the magisterium of the church."[17]

Does the Archbishop Hunthausen case show that waiting for bishops to retire in order to replace them with compliant appointees is not working fast enough for Rome? Does such action by Rome further decrease the laity's already well-documented loss of confidence in papal leadership?[18]

There may be procedures to get theologians and bishops in line. With the laity this task may be more difficult. Paul VI upheld Pius XI's and Pius XII's teaching to protect the authority of the Roman magisterium. Does not evidence show that *Humanae vitae*'s promulgation has had the opposite effect? Before the encyclical, how many Catholics would have thought that they could disagree with the pope on birth control, divorce and remarriage, and abortion and still consider themselves good Catholics? (See the results of the poll on p. ii above.)

Vatican II taught that the Holy Spirit "distributes special gifts among faithful of every rank." Newman showed how, during the fourth-century Arian heresy, it was the laity, not the bishops, who upheld the orthodox faith. At the 1980 synod Cardinal G. Emmett Carter, archbishop of Toronto, asked if this movement to a post-traditional level of reflection and concrete conduct might be a non-reflexive expression of the *sensus fidelium*.[19]

Under the Spirit's guidance, is history repeating itself: in the fourth century on dogma, today on moral issues?

---

[17]Thomas J. Reese, S.J., "The Selection of Bishops," *America*, vol. 151, no. 4 (August 25, 1984), pp. 69–71. Reese provides the confidential questionnaire used to screen out episcopal candidates who do not accept the official position on "the Ministerial Priesthood, on the priestly ordination of women, on the Sacrament of Matrimony, on sexual ethics...."

[18]According to the National Opinion Research Center at the University of Chicago (NORC), 26 percent of the drop in mass attendance from 1963 to 1973 could be attributed to loss of confidence in papal leadership.

[19]*Origins*, vol. 10, no. 18 (October 16, 1980), p. 277.

Chapter 6

Divorce and Remarriage: The Problem and the Teaching of Jesus

To the unmarried[1] and to widows I say: it is good for them to stay as
they are, like me. But if they cannot exercise self-control, let them marry,
since it is better to be married than to be burnt up.

1 Cor. 7:8–9 (New Jerusalem Bible)

Many Roman Catholics in the United States have experienced
the tragedy of divorce in their own lives or among family or
friends. Among these, many are involved in remarriage with
its attendant alienation from important aspects of church life.
This chapter will challenge the official Roman Catholic position
that the church, bound by Jesus' teaching, can do nothing to
help in these cases. The official church teaching on divorce and
remarriage is another instance of the magisterium's imposition
of a moral teaching as if it were the only legitimate option for
Catholics. We will explore the doctrine behind church policy.
We will propose that the policy has been harmful, unnecessary,
and morally unjustifiable.

How many Catholics around the world are divorced and remarried? No official figures are available. Divorce among Catholics in the United States, however, has increased from 16 percent to 24 percent in the last twenty years and the percentage is
now comparable to that among Protestants and Jews.[2]

The 1982–1986 National Opinion Research Center (NORC)
General Social Survey shows that about 26 percent of Catholics in this country have been divorced at least once.[3] Andrew

---

[1] Paul includes in this category separated couples; see v. 11.

[2] Andrew M. Greeley, *American Catholics Since the Council: An Unauthorized
Report* (Chicago: Thomas More, 1985), pp. 152–153.

[3] Letter to the author from Andrew Greeley, December 23, 1986.

Hacker reported in 1983 that 73 percent of all divorced Americans remarry.[4] It therefore seems valid to conclude that a high percentage of divorced Catholics have remarried. An unverified estimate of divorced and remarried Catholics in the United States is between six and eight million.[5]

Whatever the exact figure, very many Catholics around the world are involved. At the 1980 Synod of Bishops on the Family, the problem of divorced and remarried Catholics was "the cause of the most thought and concern for bishops from every part of the Church universal."[6]

Official Teaching

Ever since a series of decretal letters under Pope Alexander III in the twelfth century, the Roman Catholic church's official doctrine has been that a valid, consummated, sacramental marriage cannot be dissolved by any power on earth.[7] Divorced Catholics from such marriages may not remarry, and if they do, they are excluded from the sacraments (excommunicated in reality, if not in name), unless, in the most exceptional cases, they live together as "brother and sister." This official teaching prevents millions of Catholics around the world who have suffered the tragedy of broken marriages from rebuilding their lives as full-fledged church members.

In chapter 3, I noted that 26 percent of the decline in mass attendance between 1963 and 1973 could be explained by changing attitudes toward divorce. Since evidence exists that 50 percent of the divorced and remarried continue to go to mass at least once a month,[8] disaffection among Catholics over church teaching on divorce must go far beyond the divorced and remarried themselves. It would seem that many Catholics, other

---

[4] Andrew Hacker, ed., *U/S: A Statistical Portrait of the American People* (New York: Viking, 1983), p. 113.

[5] *1987 Catholic Almanac* (Huntington, Ind.: Our Sunday Visitor, 1987), p. 235.

[6] Jan Grootaers and Joseph A. Selling, *The 1980 Synod of Bishops "On the Role of the Family": Exposition of the Event and an Analysis of Its Texts,* Bibliotheca Ephemeridum Theologicarum Lovaniensium (Leuven: Leuven University Press, 1983), p. 100.

[7] Theodore Mackin, S.J., *Marriage in the Catholic Church: What Is Marriage?* (New York: Paulist, 1982), pp. 158–172.

[8] Letter from Andrew Greeley, December 23, 1986.

than those divorced, are alienated by a perception of church insensitivity to genuine human suffering, to their divorced and remarried relatives' and friends' spiritual needs.

Moreover, decline in belief and practice among Catholics cannot be explained by general religious decline in the United States during this period, since the rate of loss of practicing members among Protestants was not nearly as great as that among Catholics. In fact, a previous divorce is one of the most powerful reasons why Catholics leave the church.[9]

Official church teaching on divorce and remarriage can be found in the 1983 Code of Canon Law. It declares that all marriages are essentially monogamous and indissoluble. Canon 1056 states:

> The essential properties of marriage are unity and indissolubility, which in Christian marriage obtains a special firmness in virtue of the sacrament.

Moreover, the Code affirms that a valid marriage between baptized persons is always a sacrament.

> The matrimonial covenant... between baptized persons has been raised by Christ the Lord to the dignity of a sacrament. For this reason a matrimonial contract cannot validly exist between baptized persons unless it is also a sacrament by that fact.[10]

Notwithstanding the statement in canon 1056 on indissolubility as an essential property of marriage, marriages can be broken. Although marriage between two baptized persons is a sacrament as soon as validly ratified, it does not acquire that special firmness mentioned in canon 1055 until it has been consummated by "the conjugal act which is per se suitable for the generation of children... by which the spouses become one flesh" (canon 1061, 1). Before consummation the pope can dissolve such sacramental marriages "by the power of the keys." Non-Christian marriages can also be dissolved under "Pauline privilege" if one spouse enters the church (1 Cor. 7:12–15).

---

[9]Andrew M. Greeley, *Crisis in the Church* (Chicago: Thomas More, 1979), p. 130.

[10]Canon 1055, 1 and 2.

In addition, under what is known as "Petrine privilege," the pope has dissolved consummated, non-sacramental marriages between baptized and unbaptized spouses "in favor of the faith."

Therefore, it can be said quite explicitly that, in Roman Catholic teaching, only Christians' valid, ratified, consummated marriages can never be dissolved by any power on earth. Official doctrine holds that this is God's will, revealed in Jesus' explicit teaching and developed in the church's living tradition.

Annulments

The church has courts called marriage tribunals to deal with broken marriages; while it denies the possibility of divorce for those in validly consummated Christian marriage, these courts grant what are called annulments. Just as civil courts throw out contracts where essential elements have not been fulfilled, so marriage tribunals issue decrees of nullity where essential requirements of a valid marriage can be proven not to have been present at the time of marriage. Only after receiving a decree of nullity can Catholics involved in broken marriages remarry in the church.

James Provost, chairman of the canon law faculty at Catholic University, studied annulments in 1975 to find out how well the system works.[11] Provost's examination distinguished between two different types of marriage cases: conflict situations and hardship cases.

Conflict cases are those in which necessary requirements of a true marriage have not been fulfilled. In these cases, if facts can be proven, tribunals can grant an annulment. Provost's first conclusion about these conflict cases is that they result in relief for very few Catholics throughout the world. According to the church's General Statistics Office, 95 percent of all cases that received *any* hearing, whether the outcome was favorable or unfavorable, were reported from Europe, Canada, the United States, Colombia, and Australia.

With divorce statistics from the United Nations and nullification figures from the Vatican, Provost estimated that only about 7.5 percent of potential cases reached diocesan marriage

---

[11] James H. Provost, "Intolerable Marriage Situations Revisited," *The Jurist: Studies in Church Law and Ministry,* vol. 40, no. 1 (1980), pp. 153–154.

tribunals around the world. Tribunal effectiveness in caring for the potential caseload ranged from 0.4 percent in France to 11.5 percent in Italy.[12]

American diocesan tribunals rendered decisions in 10 percent of the cases of people with a right to a hearing. Although there were an estimated 225,720 divorces affecting Catholics in the United States in 1975, diocesan marriage tribunals handed down only 23,034 decisions. With over 200,000 cases a year not considered, this would result in over 2 million unaddressed cases in a ten-year period. So an estimate of six to eight million Catholics in the United States involved in this tragic situation does not seem exaggerated.

We have no reason to hope that divorces among Catholics will decrease in the foreseeable future. Nor does the drop in priestly vocations and shortage of funds and personnel make likely any increase in the number of annulments granted to those who are entitled to them.

Moreover, John Paul II wants the number of annulments reduced. A news item headed "Too Many Annulments" reads:

> Speaking to the 25 judges of the Rota John Paul II deplored "the excessive proliferation and almost automatic annulments of marriages on pretexts of immaturity or diminished responsibility." Tribunals must not "become an easy way of finding a solution for failed marriages and irregular arrangements for marriage partners." The pope deplored the drift toward a sort of Catholic divorce and warned judges to watch out for those who presented their "slight mental troubles" or moral weakness as "proof of inability to carry out their conjugal obligations."[13]

Hardship cases are those in which the marriage was clearly valid, but is now irretrievably broken. Here, marriage tribunals can do nothing. According to official, contemporary Roman Catholic teaching these marriages can be dissolved only by the death of a spouse. Can anything be said about the official claim that the indissolubility of valid, consummated, sacramental marriages

---

[12]In 1975, Italy had no provision for civil divorce. Only the church courts could grant any kind of relief for broken marriages.

[13]*The Tablet*, vol. 241, no. 7649 (January 14, 1987), p. 177.

is both the clear teaching of Jesus and the church's firm and constant tradition that cannot be changed?

As we shall see, neither scripture nor the first thousand years of tradition supports official teaching that such marriages can be dissolved only by one of the spouses' death. Evidence from scripture is uncertain and has been interpreted in different ways from the church's earliest years. As for tradition, a continuous, firm tradition in the Eastern church, from long before the break between East and West, permits remarriage, especially of the innocent party, after a broken marriage. In the Western church, the discipline against remarriage was not firmly established until the twelfth century

At the 1980 Synod of Bishops on the Family there was a strong demand, ignored by Pope John Paul II, to study the practice of the Orthodox Church. That church, in consideration of human weakness, continues to tolerate remarriage and reception of the Eucharist, although it does not consider the second marriage a sacrament.

What Did Jesus Teach?

Consider evidence from scripture. Differences among biblical texts and widely divergent attempts to interpret them indicate lack of support in scripture for the present discipline.

In *Divorce and Remarriage,* Theodore Mackin, S.J., devotes forty-six pages to a discussion of texts and the complex and often contradictory scholarly attempts to interpret them.[14] The late George W. MacRae, S.J., observed that no single interpretation of these texts has won general consent of exegetes, at least Catholic ones, and, perhaps for this reason, the church has never attempted to define their sense.[15]

Biblical texts do not unequivocally show that, during his ministry, Jesus taught an absolute prohibition against divorce and remarriage. Nor was any absolute prohibition upheld in the primitive church. In the most conservative interpretation, biblical texts show a church already adapting Jesus' teaching to

---

[14]Theodore Mackin, S.J., *Divorce and Remarriage* (New York: Paulist, 1984), pp. 43–89.

[15]George W. MacRae, S.J., *Studies in New Testament and Gnosticism* (Wilmington: Michael Glazier, 1987), pp. 115–129.

human needs during the period when the scriptures were being written.

Official doctrine on the absolute indissolubility of a consummated, valid marriage between two baptized Christians is based on the teaching of Jesus as transmitted in Paul's First Letter to the Corinthians and in the synoptic Gospels. The earliest account is that of Paul. The apostle first states what he had learned from tradition:

> To the married I proclaim — it is not I who do so, but the Lord — that the wife is not to be separated from her husband. And if she is in fact separated, she is either to remain unmarried or is to be reconciled to her husband. And a husband is not to dismiss his wife.
> (1 Cor. 7:10–11; Mackin's translation)[16]

Paul then on his own authority proceeds to modify that teaching to fit the needs of believers in his own churches:

> To the rest I say, not the Lord... if the unbelieving partner desires to separate, let it be so; in such a case the brother or sister is not bound. For God has called us to peace.
> (1 Cor. 7:12–15)

Paul adapted what he received as Jesus' original teaching to a missionary situation. In his churches, pagans sometimes abandoned spouses who had been converted. Paul allowed abandoned converts to marry again.

Synoptic Gospels

Luke: "Everyone who dismisses his wife and marries another commits adultery, and he who marries a woman dismissed from her husband commits adultery." (Luke 16:18)

Mark: "Whoever dismisses his wife and marries another, commits adultery against her, and if she dismisses her husband and marries another, she commits adultery." (Mark 10:11–12)

Matthew: "Whoever dismisses his wife, except for unchastity [*porneia*], and marries another commits adultery [*moicheia*]." (Matt. 19:9, cf. Matt. 5:32).

---

[16]See Jerome Murphy-O'Connor, O.P., *1 Corinthians* (Wilmington: Michael Glazier, 1979), p. 63, on mistranslation of this passage in the Revised Standard Version (RSV).

Because Luke mentions only the situation of a husband who dismisses his wife,[17] widely held opinion finds this close to Jesus' original teaching, since his audience consisted of Jews, among whom only the husband could get a divorce. Mark would then have adapted the original teaching of Jesus to fit a Roman audience among whom either husbands or wives could obtain a divorce.

Although most scholars consider the Lucan divorce saying an absolute prohibition against divorce, there is, as we shall see below, a quite plausible way of understanding Jesus' saying in Luke that would not support an absolute prohibition against all divorce.

With Matthew, attempts to recover Jesus' exact teaching become even more problematical. Matthew twice states an exception. "Whoever dismisses his wife, except for unchastity [*porneia*], and marries another commits adultery [*moicheia*]" (Matt. 19:9; cf. Matt. 5:32). During many centuries *porneia* has been understood to mean adultery. The teaching of the Orthodox church, namely, that the husband who dismisses an adulterous wife can remarry, is based on Matthew.

Fitzmyer and some other modern scholars deny that the word *porneia,* in the exceptive clause, means "adultery" (*moicheia*).[18] They are convinced that *porneia* refers, not to adultery, but to incestuous marriages, that is, marriages with close kin, common among pagans but forbidden in Leviticus 18:6–18. This interpretation assumes that Jewish Christians in the Matthean church would have been gravely offended if Gentile Christians were allowed to remain in marriages considered incestuous in the law of Moses.

MacRae and others disagree with this recently developed interpretation.[19] Since *porneia* refers to "every kind of unlawful

---

[17]Most contemporary translations render *apolyōn,* "divorces." However, Mackin suggests that "'dismisses' reflects more accurately the Rabbinic form of 'divorce' — a unilateral act by the husband, not a decree by an authoritative body." Note from Mackin to author.

[18]Joseph A. Fitzmyer, S.J., "The Matthean Divorce Texts and Some New Palestinian Evidence," *Theological Studies,* vol. 37, no. 2 (June 1976), pp. 197–226.

[19]The earliest reference in Fitzmyer's article is to W.K.L. Clarke, "The Excepting Clause in St. Matthew," *Theology* 15 (1927). For rejection of the incest theory see Georg Strecker, *The Sermon on the Mount: An Exegetical Commentary,* trans. O. C. Dean, Jr. (Nashville: Abingdon, 1988), p. 203, n. 29.

sexual intercourse," as well as to "the sexual unfaithfulness of a married woman,"[20] the evangelist may have chosen *porneia* precisely to broaden the kind of unchastity that can break a marriage.

However one interprets *porneia,* Matthew sought to ease tensions in a community with many Jewish Christians living with Gentile Christians.

Another difficulty, however, arises because Jesus' teaching in Mark and Matthew is based on Genesis and would therefore apply to all human marriages, not just Christian ones. Jesus had been challenged by Pharisees who quoted Moses' permission to write a certificate of divorce. Jesus referred them to God's plan in Genesis in order to reject Moses' permissive attitude toward divorce:

> But from the beginning of creation *he made them male and female. This is why a man leaves his father and mother, and the two become one flesh.* They are no longer two, therefore, but one flesh. So then, what God has united, human beings must not divide. (Mark 10:6–9, NJB)

If Jesus intended to establish an absolute prohibition against all divorce based on God's plan "from the beginning of creation," it would apply to the entire human race. How can one justify Paul's exception or the current church policy of dissolving non-Christian marriages?[21]

Of Jesus' saying "human beings must not divide," Lawrence Wrenn, judge on the Hartford matrimonial tribunal, comments that Jesus could have said that what God has united no one *is able* to divide. This would have made clear the existence of an unbreakable bond. Rather, "let not" suggests that the marriage can be broken but should not be.[22] Wrenn thinks Jesus taught

---

[20]Walter Bauer, *A Greek-English Lexicon of the New Testament and Other Christian Literature,* trans. and ed. William F. Arndt and F. Wilbur Gingrich, 4th ed. (Chicago: University of Chicago Press, 1952), pp. 699–700.

[21]St. Ambrose later tried to solve the problem of Paul's exception by saying that only Christian marriage is from God (Mackin, *Divorce and Remarriage,* p. 158).

[22]"The Greek verb *mēchōrizétō* is plainly the *hortative* subjunctive after the negative participle" (Mackin).

that a bond existed, but that it is fragile and care should be taken not to break it.[23]

Difficulty also arises from the position of the divorce clause in the Sermon on the Mount. In a series of six sayings on anger, lust, divorce, oath taking, resisting evil, and love of enemies, only the saying on divorce has been absolutized by the church into a binding law. The other five sayings are considered ideals to be worked toward.

Another Interpretation of the Divorce Passages

I believe that our interpretation of these texts from Paul and the synoptic Gospels has been influenced by seven centuries of teaching on divorce and remarriage in the Western church. We have read back into the scriptures a meaning needed to support the Latin church's present discipline.

If we were to take a less partisan approach to the Gospels, we would begin with Mark, widely accepted as the first Gospel to be written and a source for Matthew and Luke. Mark's Gospel has been called a passion narrative with a long introduction. The author deliberately organized his story to show how, almost from the beginning of Jesus' ministry, opposition built leading to his passion and death. Already in chapter 3, his opponents made plans to destroy him.

Part of this lethal antagonism can be found in the "entrapment stories." His enemies tried to trap Jesus with questions about dangerous or controversial issues. They would put him in a position where no matter how he answered, he would antagonize and lose the support of those on one side or the other of the controversy. Best known of these stories involved payment of taxes to Caesar. If he answered: "Yes," he would alienate people who hated the Roman occupation. If he answered: "No," he would be in jeopardy with the Roman authorities.

I suggest that the question about divorce is just such a trap to catch him on an issue on which there was serious disagreement between two schools of thought among Pharisees. Shammai allowed divorce only for a serious fault in the wife; Hillel

---

[23]Lawrence G. Wrenn, "Marriage — Indissoluble or Fragile?" in Lawrence G. Wrenn, ed., *Divorce and Remarriage in the Catholic Church* (New York: Newman Press, 1972), p. 135.

permitted divorce for lesser reasons.[24] So a trap was set to catch Jesus between these two groups. "And the Pharisees came up and in order to test him asked, 'Is it lawful for a man to divorce his wife?'" (Mark 10:2).

In the Jewish society of that time there were only two places where a woman could live in decent respectability: in her father's house until marriage and in her husband's house after marriage. "For emancipated women there was in the ancient world only one calling."[25]

Jesus' answer to the two disputing parties ("For your hardness of heart Moses allowed you to dismiss your wives, but from the beginning it was not so"; Matt. 19:8; see Mark 10:5) could well be a rejection of the whole controversy as involving a callous attitude toward women. His purpose could have been not to lay down a law establishing the absolute indissolubility of marriage, but to protect women in the social situation of his day from men's ability, for one reason or another, to throw their wives out and thus make them social outcasts.

Sayings in both Matthew (5:32; 19:9) and Luke (16:18) can be seen to agree with such an interpretation of Jesus' intention. In none can be found a word of condemnation of the wife. Jesus accuses only the husband who casts out his wife and the man who takes advantage of her sad situation. In like manner, Paul speaks of what is not to be done to a wife. A correct translation of Paul — "that a wife is not to be separated [passive voice] from her husband.... And a husband is not to dismiss his wife" (1 Cor. 7:10) — yields a similar understanding of Jesus' intention, that men must not abuse their wives by sending them away.[26]

Paul (1 Cor. 7:10–11), Matthew (5:32; 19:9), and Luke (16:18) yield a consistent interpretation that accords with the situation described by Mark. Jesus' concern may have been to protect women rather than to safeguard the stability of marriage through an absolute law against divorce. Mark adapted Jesus' original teaching to a Roman situation where there would be

---

[24] *Jerome Biblical Commentary,* 68:120.

[25] George Foot Moore, *Judaism in the First Centuries of the Christian Era,* vol. 2 (New York: Schocken, 1971), pp. 126–127.

[26] The Greek *choristhênai* is in the passive "not to be separated," which implies an action taken against her, not as in the RSV "should not separate from her husband," which suggests an action that she initiates.

greater equality between men and women in obtaining divorces. Mark has, however, kept the divorce saying in the context of the attempt to trap Jesus, which makes possible this interpretation of Jesus' intention.

But, some will say, perhaps Jesus intended to protect women and the family by laying down an absolute prohibition of divorce. This is doubtful. Both Paul and Matthew would then be guilty of providing exceptions to what they had received as the Lord's absolute prohibition. It is true that the exceptions could be ascribed to the Spirit of the Risen Lord who spoke through Christian prophets. But would we not more plausibly recognize the Spirit's work in the exceptions if we do not insist that Jesus during his ministry laid down an absolute prohibition against all divorce based on a divine plan revealed in Genesis?

Has enough attention been given to the psychological implications of the exceptions in Paul and Matthew? Paul wrote about thirty years after Jesus taught. The Matthean exception "except for unchastity" is usually attributed to the evangelist and would have been written between fifty and sixty years after the events described. In such a short period of time, would Paul and Matthew change a teaching of Jesus transmitted to them as clear and unequivocal? A reading of the Jesus saying, however, that does not involve an absolute prohibition of divorce makes the exceptions psychologically consistent with Jesus' concern for women.

A strong consensus holds that both Matthew and Luke wrote with Mark's Gospel available to them. Why did Luke leave out the entrapment story in Mark's Gospel and keep only a saying on divorce? A possible explanation is that his independent tradition led him to question the story's historical accuracy. Especially noteworthy, if his intention was to teach absolute indissolubility, is Luke's omission of Jesus' purported saying, "What therefore God has joined together, let not man put asunder" (Mark 10:9; Matt. 19:6b).

In view of Luke's omission, can we be sure that the passage from Genesis was actually quoted by Jesus? But, even if it was, we no longer quote Jesus to support the historicity of the story of Jonah and the whale or use opening chapters of Genesis for scientific information about the creation of the world or the origin of the species.

Some caution is justified in building a complete theology of marriage, binding for all times and all cultural situations, on a few verses from Genesis and a purported saying of Jesus reported only by Mark and Matthew. Genesis may or may not have been quoted by Jesus, and "human beings must not divide" can have more than one interpretation. Jesus' divorce saying in Luke may be a demand that wives not be abused, rather than promulgation of an absolute, eternally binding law on divorce and remarriage.[27]

In view of these differing interpretations of scriptural evidence, is it not reasonable to say that we simply do not have certainty about Jesus' teaching on divorce and remarriage? We saw that Paul thought the Spirit guided his deliberate adaptation of a tradition that he believed had come from the Lord. If the Matthean exception, namely "except on the ground of unchastity [*porneia*]" is to be attributed to the evangelist, then he also seems to have made a conscious exception.

Biblical evidence for Jesus' teaching on divorce does not support the church's present discipline on divorce and remarriage. Uncertainty about that teaching and its implication for consciences has continued in church tradition down to our own time. That tradition must now be examined.

---

[27]For a popularly written analysis that reaches a similar conclusion using form-criticism see Tübingen New Testament scholar Gerhard Lohfink, *The Bible: Now I Get It! A Form-Criticism Handbook,* trans. Daniel Coogan (Garden City: Doubleday, 1979), pp. 142–151.

Chapter 7

Divorce and Remarriage: Tradition and Change

> He who cannot keep continence after the death of his wife, or who has separated from his wife for a valid motive, as fornication, adultery, or another misdeed, if he takes another wife, or if the wife takes another husband, the divine word does not condemn them or exclude them from the Church or the life; but she tolerates it rather on account of their weakness. *— St. Epiphanius of Cyprus*

In chapter 6 we noted the official church claim that the current Roman Catholic discipline on divorce and remarriage can never be changed because it is based on the clear teaching of Jesus, as developed in tradition. But we also saw that Jesus' teaching does not lend itself to a single interpretation. The uncertainty in scripture continued in the early church tradition and in the attempts of modern scholars to interpret that tradition. In his 1984 study, Theodore Mackin, S.J., concluded that the early church allowed remarriage after divorce. To the accusation of Henri Crouzel that he had prejudged the evidence, Mackin responded: "By the time I started writing I had in fact made up my mind. But I had not done so when starting to examine the evidence. The examination made up my mind."[1]

The evidence reveals uncertainty among early Christian writers attempting to apply the teaching of Paul and the Gospels in the Roman Empire, with its easy consensual divorce. Influenced by Stoic idealism, early church Fathers taught that marriage should be absolutely monogamous. Indeed, Athenagoras and Tertullian, after he joined the heretical Montanist sect, even considered marriage in widowhood adulterous.

But even while they sought to promote a high ideal of monogamous marriage, Christian writers always had to contend with

---

[1] Letter to the author, December 31, 1986. See Theodore Mackin, S.J., *Divorce and Remarriage* (New York: Paulist, 1984), p. 139 n. 3.

Paul's exception (1 Cor. 7:10–11) and the exception given twice in Matthew (5:32; 19:9).

The Early Church Fathers

The ambiguity appears in writings of the Latin church Father *Tertullian* (c. 155–220). Before joining the Montanists, Tertullian wrote two books on marriage for his wife. In the first he urged her not to remarry in case of his death, but to embrace the holiness of a life of continence. But in the second book, since second marriages could not be absolutely condemned, Tertullian asked that she at least not marry a pagan. He warned her against recent examples of women who, *after divorce* or their husband's death, not only rejected an excellent opportunity to lead lives of continence, but married pagans. For Tertullian, their fault seems not to have been remarriage after divorce, but marrying pagans.[2]

In a controversy with Marcion, Tertullian insisted that Jesus' condemnation of divorce was conditional. He wrote:

> Thus if Christ has forbidden one to dismiss a spouse under a certain condition, he has not forbidden it entirely. And that which he has not forbidden entirely, he has otherwise permitted, when the reason for his forbidding it ceases.[3]

Yet in Book 5 of the same work, Tertullian seemed indecisive about what he had just written. Later, in fact, he condemned remarriage under any circumstances.[4]

Around 240, *Origen* of Alexandria wrote that

> apart from or contrary to the scriptures certain heads of the Church have permitted a certain woman to be [re-]married while her husband is still alive.... However they have not acted altogether unreasonably. This accommodation is allowed in lieu of even worse ones....[5]

---

[2] *Ad uxorem*, II:1, *CCSL*, 1 (Turnholt, 1957), pp. 381–382.
[3] *Adversus Marcionem*, IV, 4, *CCSL*, 1:365.
[4] *De exhortatione castitatis*, ch. 5.
[5] *In Matthaeum commentarii*, 14, 23; *PG* 10, 781.

Whether Origen approved or disapproved of these concessions, he surely reported actions of bishops in his own church. Moreover, it is inconceivable in the social conditions of the time that such concessions were granted to women and not to men.

As Mackin notes, witnesses from about 180 to about 380 in both East and West, with almost no exceptions, make clear that a man dismissing an adulterous wife and remarrying could receive communion without having to do penance. Since this permission applied only to the husband, widespread acceptance of a literal interpretation of the Matthean exception must be the explanation.

Around 380, Eastern and Western churches diverged in their treatment of divorce and remarriage. The East used the letters of Basil the Great (d. 379) to support a practice — still in force in the Orthodox Church — to allow remarriage after divorce.

In the West a different tradition began to develop with the teaching of Ambrose (d. 397), Jerome (d. 420), and Augustine (d. 430). It became the foundation for the Western church's eventual affirmation in the twelfth century of the absolute indissolubility of Christian marriage. Note that the contemporary difference in discipline between Roman Catholics and Orthodox began to develop many centuries before the Great Schism. Indeed Basil, author of the Eastern canons, is listed as one of Ambrose's favorite authors and an influential source of his theological knowledge.[6] Had Basil's letters been better known in the West, would separate traditions on divorce and remarriage have developed?

Current difference in discipline on divorce and remarriage in Roman Catholic and Orthodox churches influences interpretation of the ancient texts. The problem begins with two of the "Canonical Letters" of *Basil the Great.*[7] In canon 4, Basil described the penitential discipline for the twice-married and the thrice-married before they could be admitted to communion.[8] Father John Meyendorff, Russian Orthodox historian and the-

---

[6] F. Homes Dudden, *The Life and Times of St. Ambrose,* vol. 1 (Oxford: Clarendon Press, 1935), p. 113.

[7] Source of sixty-eight canons later included in the canons of the Eastern church. See *St. Basil: Letters,* vol. 2, trans. Sister Agnes Clare Way, C.D.P., with notes by Roy J. Deferrari in *The Fathers of the Church: A New Translation* (New York: Fathers of the Church, 1955), p. xiii.

[8] Ibid., pp. 14–15.

ologian, states that "twice-married" refers to those "who enter marriage after either widowhood or divorce."[9] Roy J. Deferrari, Roman Catholic classical scholar at Catholic University and editor of *The Fathers of the Church,* has a footnote to "twice-married," which reads: "Those who have married after the death of their first spouse."[10] The text reads only *digamoi,* twice-married. Which scholar is giving the text's true meaning and which is reading back into Basil's canon his own church's present discipline? The contradiction illustrates the ambiguity of interpretations plaguing discussion of divorce and remarriage from the beginning and throws doubt on those who would insist on clarity of scripture and tradition on the subject.

In the more frequently cited canon 35, Basil wrote:

> About an abandoned husband, one must first examine the reason for his being abandoned. If it appears that his wife left him without cause, he merits being pardoned, she being punished. The pardon is accorded to the husband so that he may be in communion with the Church.[11]

Although Deferrari's interpretation of canon 4 may be correct, his interpretation of canon 35 is harder to justify. In his footnote to canon 35, Deferrari refers to commentaries of Zonaras, the major twelfth-century Byzantine historian and canonist, and his successor, Aristenus. Deferrari correctly notes that Zonaras, who as the Greek text makes clear is not concerned with the question of remarriage, says of the man separated from his wife that "he is not to be separated from the Church, but he may not *cohabit* with another woman. Cf. Zonaras, *PG* 138:702" (emphasis added).

But Deferrari's discussion of Aristenus's commentary is not accurate. He writes:

> According to Aristenus... the sense is that, even if he *lives with another woman* [*labēi gynaika*], he is to be pardoned, that is, he is not to be subjected to the punishment for adultery. (emphasis added)

---

[9]John Meyendorff, *Marriage: An Orthodox Perspective,* 2nd ed. (Crestwood, N.Y.: St. Vladimir's Seminary Press, 1975), p. 49.

[10]In *St. Basil: Letters,* p. 14, n. 44.

[11]*St. Basil: Letters,* Letter 199, pp. 57–58.

Deferrari's literal translation of *labēi gynaika* as "lives with another woman" distorts Aristenus's meaning. It implies the kind of permissive cohabitation that Zonaras had rejected. Aristenus's meaning is accurately expressed in the Latin text of Migne: *duxerit uxorem*, "takes a wife," which means precisely entering into another marriage. The reference to Aristenus should have read: "According to Aristenus...the sense is that, even if he married another woman, he is to be pardoned, that is, he is not to be subjected to the punishment for adultery."

Deferrari's inaccurate translation makes Basil and his medieval Orthodox commentators consistent with the discipline of the modern Western church.

Any doubt about the meaning is completely absent in St. Epiphanius of Cyprus (d. 403), who wrote about the same time:

He who cannot keep continence after the death of his wife, or who has separated from his wife for a valid motive, as fornication, adultery, or another misdeed, if he takes another wife, or if the wife takes another husband, the divine word does not condemn them or exclude them from the Church or the life; but she tolerates it rather on account of their weakness.[12]

This has been the discipline of the Orthodox Church to the present day.

Evidence from other Fathers of East and West in the fourth century is equivocal. When Gregory of Nazianzus and John Chrysostom in the East and Ambrose in the West dealt with marriage, especially in their sermons on Matthew or 1 Corinthians, they did not comment on the exceptions. They seemed to come up to the issue and then back away. Ambrose had a brief statement in his commentary on Luke, which suggested that a marriage was dissolved by adultery, but said nothing in that commentary about the possibility of remarriage.

How can one explain this reluctance of the Fathers to face a question that must have been just as practical for them as for us: Can the spouse who has dismissed an adulterous spouse remarry? It is possible that they were reacting to the Stoic ideal that rejected remarriage even in widowhood as a yielding to lust.

---

[12]*Against heresies,* 69, *PG 41,* col. 1024C–1025A.

We saw in chapter 4 that early Christian writers insisted that the Christian ideal was as high as the Stoic. Some said even higher. Did they think that the exception in Matthew pointed to a lesser ideal, which they decided to ignore?

The Western Tradition

A tradition of absolute indissolubility, which finally prevailed in the West, begins with *Ambrose* and his short treatise *De Abraham*. In his baptismal instruction he clearly rejected remarriage after divorce: "You are bound to a wife; do not seek for a dissolution, for you are forbidden to take another wife as long as your first wife lives." Attempting to cover an adulterous relationship with legal respectability through a divorce only added to the sin's gravity.[13]

Jerome, in his *Commentary on Matthew,* also seems to deny that the exceptive clause in Matthew allowed the husband to remarry. But Augustine became the principal source for the teaching, ultimately adopted in the Western church, that Christian marriages could not be dissolved.

Augustine spoke of the existence of an unbreakable "bond." In 401 he wrote that the marriage bond is so strong that for Christians, even after divorce, spouses remained joined to one another. He concluded, however, that this was true only for Christians, that is, "only in the City of God, in his Holy Mountain," Augustine's designation for the church.[14] This supports the Roman Catholic church's present teaching that only the marriages of the baptized are absolutely indissoluble.

Augustine also served as a source for the later use of Ephesians 5 to justify the indissolubility of marriage.[15] No evidence exists in Ephesians that its author had any concern about divorce. His purpose lay in showing God's eternal plan of reconciliation, God's *mystérion.* As that "mystery" is worked out in Christian life, Christ's love for the church becomes the model for love between husband and wife. As Markus Barth points out, however: "In Eph 5 Paul gives no indication whether he

---

[13]*De Abraham,* I:7, *PL* 14, col. 442.
[14]*De Bono Coniugali, PL,* 40, col. 379.
[15]Theodore Mackin, S.J., "Ephesians 5:21–33 and Radical Indissolubility," *Marriage Studies: Reflections in Canon Law and Theology* 3 (1985), pp. 1–45.

would have resisted and condemned divorce between members of the church under any circumstances."[16]

Use of Ephesians 5:22–33 as a proof text to deny the possibility of divorce for married Christians seems to begin with Augustine's use of verse 32. A translation of the Greek reads: "This mystery [*mystérion*] is a great one (I say this in reference to Christ and the church)."[17] Augustine, however, using the Latin Vulgate where the Greek *mystérion* is rendered *sacramentum*, wrote:

> "This is a great *sacramentum*," says the Apostle, "in Christ and in the Church (Ephesians 5:32)." Therefore that which is great in Christ and in the Church is quite small in each and every husband and wife, but is the *sacramentum* of inseparable union.[18]

Augustine identified this "sign," that is, *sacramentum*, as the marital bond itself, which can be broken only by death.

Later theologians reasoned that because the bond between Christ and the church can never be broken, so the bond between husband and wife cannot be broken. They transformed a metaphor in Ephesians into law.[19]

Not every bishop accepted Augustine's teaching on absolute indissolubility. Augustine responded in *De adulterinis coniugiis* to another African bishop, Pollentius, who affirmed that in the case of adultery the innocent spouse could obtain a divorce unilaterally and remarry. With a complicated exegesis unacceptable to modern scholars, Augustine demolished Pollentius's position. Canon 8 of the Eleventh Council of Carthage included Augustine's teaching and requested its adoption in imperial law. In general the opposition to remarriage after divorce was based in

---

[16]Markus Barth, *Ephesians: Translation and Commentary on Chapters 4–6,* Anchor Bible 34A (New York: Doubleday, 1974), p. 703 n. 268.

[17]Mackin's translation.

[18]*De Nuptiis et Concupiscentia,* I:21, *PL 44,* col. 1427.

[19]Mackin, "Ephesians 5:21–33 and Radical Indissolubility," p. 45. "Paul's analogy, Christ-Church/husband-wife, he intended as a model of the love to which he exhorted Christian spouses. At the most the link between the two marital relationships (one metaphoric, the other real) is *deontological,* i.e., the earthly love union *ought* to be indissoluble. To make the link *ontological,* i.e., the earthly union *is* indissoluble and is *made so* by the metaphoric Christ-Church marriage, is an unwarranted logical leap." Note to author.

concern for the sexual opportunities that remarriage afforded and was part of a general effort by church authorities to restrict sexual activity.[20]

Imperial law provides evidence of a different Christian attitude toward divorce and remarriage from this same period. Christianity had become the official imperial religion and Christian Roman law continued for centuries to permit dissolution of marriage by the spouses' mutual consent. Christian emperors, from Constantine in 331 to Justinian in 566, all sincerely sought to make Christianity the law of the empire. Although they sought to discourage its widespread practice, they consistently allowed consensual divorce, with its right of remarriage. These Christian emperors surely knew that some theologians taught the indissolubility of marriage. Yet for over two hundred years of imperial legislation there was no thought that remarriage after divorce was evil or invalid.[21] The Council of Carthage's request was ignored. Christians in good faith could believe marriage to be dissoluble or indissoluble without fear of being considered heretics. Calm acceptance of marriage as dissoluble in Roman law from 331 to 566 is clear evidence that the indissolubility of marriage had not yet been definitively established.

Unsettled Questions

Official teaching on indissolubility holds that the doctrine is the will of God revealed in scripture and tradition. It is claimed that the doctrine is explicitly contained in the teaching of Christ in the synoptic Gospels and in St. Paul, and finally worked out in the church's living tradition. But careful examination has shown that evidence from scripture is uncertain and early patristic evidence continues that uncertainty.

Historically, two different traditions have developed, one in the East and one in the West. I have suggested that during the age of Basil and Epiphanius in the East and Ambrose, Jerome, and Augustine in the West the two traditions divided. But in an

---

[20]James A. Brundage, *Law, Sex and Christian Society in Medieval Europe,* (Chicago: University of Chicago Press, 1987), p. 97.

[21]John T. Noonan, Jr., "Novel 22," in William W. Bassett, ed. *The Bond of Marriage* (Notre Dame: University of Notre Dame Press, 1968), p. 75. See Brundage, *Law, Sex and Christian Society in Medieval Europe,* pp. 114–117.

important sense this is not true. It is true that the East, under the reasonably stable conditions of the empire, supported Basil's teaching, maintained in the Orthodox church to our day. In the West, however, centuries passed before a single tradition was established.

Among the Western Fathers only Ambrosiaster clearly said yes to the question about remarriage. His commentary on 1 Corinthians 7 granted permission to remarry to husbands who dismissed adulterous wives, but not to wives of adulterous husbands. Thought to be the work of Ambrose of Milan, the commentary was finally recognized in the sixteenth century to be that of an otherwise unknown fifth-century exegete. His opinion kept the case for indissolubility unsettled in the West for centuries.

Decisions of two popes provide an interesting contrast. In the fifth century, Leo I addressed the case of thousands of soldiers taken captive whose wives had legally remarried. Asked what was to be done if their husbands returned, he replied that it was "necessary that the legitimate union be restored."[22] Almost two centuries later in a letter to Boniface, Gregory II wrote:

> You have asked what is a husband to do if his wife, having been afflicted with an infirmity, cannot have intercourse with the husband. It would be good if he could remain as he is and practice abstinence. But since this requires great virtue, if he cannot live chastely, it is better if he marry. Let him not stop supporting her.[23]

After the sack of Rome in 410, central authority broke down dramatically. Decrees of local councils, anonymous writers of penitentials (handbooks used by priests to determine the penances to impose on repentant sinners), and writings of local canonists are our principal sources of information during several centuries. Two synods of Patrick and his suffragan bishops, held in Ireland between 450 and 460, are of special interest because they occurred before the Irish churches were romanized. Both

---

[22] *Epistola* 94; *PL*, 54:1136–1137.

[23] Lawrence G. Wrenn, "Marriage — Indissoluble or Fragile?" in Lawrence G. Wrenn, ed., *Divorce and Remarriage in the Catholic Church* (New York: Newman Press, 1972), p. 138. Was this an "unconsummated" marriage? See Brundage, *Law, Sex and Christian Society in Medieval Europe*, pp. 143–144.

allowed remarriage after dismissal of an adulterous wife. Local councils of Frankish bishops in 755 and 756 listed several cases in which the innocent husband could remarry, including the case of a spouse's contracting leprosy.

But change was on the way. The Synod of Aachen, held in Charlemagne's palace in 789, simply quoted the Eleventh Council of Carthage, canon 8, with Augustine's teaching forbidding remarriage after the dismissal of a spouse. Then, in 796 at the Council of Friuli in northern Italy, for the first time a council taught explicitly that the innocent husband who dismissed his wife for adultery was not only forbidden to remarry, but was declared incapable of remarrying while his first wife lived. To justify their teaching, the bishops appealed to "that most expert and blessed man, Jerome," in his *Commentary on Matthew.* As late as 1031, however, the Synod of Bourges allowed remarriage after separation because of adultery.[24]

By the end of the eleventh century, as evident in the writings of Ivo, bishop of Chartres, Augustine became an authoritative source. In his *Decretum,* the most comprehensive compilation of sources up to his time, Ivo ignored the Eastern Fathers. Typical of selective use of scripture by Ivo and other writers is their failure to mention Matthew.

The Western Position Solidified

To appreciate the significant contributions of two twelfth-century scholars, Gratian, the canonist, and Peter Lombard, the theologian, to the final form of the Roman Catholic church's law, we may recall how narrowly present church law defines which marriages are indissoluble. In spite of canon 1056 of the Code of Canon Law on indissolubility as an essential property of marriage, the Code carefully leaves an opening for some marriages to be more indissoluble than others. It continues by saying that in Christian marriages this indissolubility "obtains an added firmness in virtue of the sacrament."

By Gratian's time, unconsummated Christian marriages were being dissolved by religious vows or by papal dispensation. To account for these exceptions to absolute indissolubility, Gratian distinguished between two stages in which marriage, now viewed

---

[24]Ibid., p. 201.

as a contract, came into being. The first stage is the exchange of final consent, which creates a true but inchoate marriage. This inchoate marriage becomes indissoluble only at the second stage, consummation, when the two have become one flesh.

Lombard also contributed to the teaching that a consummated, *sacramental* marriage is absolutely indissoluble. Using Augustine's teaching on the three ends of marriage, fidelity, offspring, and *sacramentum,* he wrote that *sacramentum* makes marriage indissoluble, because it is an image of the union of Christ and the church, a union that can never be broken. The elements of the Western church's present discipline were in place, ready to be fixed:

> Only a marriage that is a sacrament is indissoluble, because it alone images the unbreakable union of Christ and the Church. And only a marriage that is consummated as well as a sacrament is indissoluble, because it alone images that union truly and completely.[25]

Since nearly everyone in Western Christendom was baptized, canon lawyers had reduced the possibility of dissolution to cases of non-consummation, which they could carefully control.

Without a strong central authority to enforce the discipline, however, the scholars' work might have had no effect, and scholarly debate on the issues could have swung back toward a more benign interpretation. A strong reforming papacy intent on control in sexual matters kept that from happening.

Why was a rigid discipline adopted in spite of (1) the Matthean exception, (2) several centuries of diverse teaching and practice in the West, and (3) contrary development in the East? I believe it was due in part to important characteristic differences between the authorities that enforced discipline in East and West.

In the church's early history in the Roman Empire, civil regulation of the legal aspects of marriage had been accepted by the church in East and West alike. Destruction of Western imperial power by barbarian invasions did not affect civil authority in the East. Civil courts continued to control legal aspects of marriage and divorce in their own territory. So no special church courts

---

[25]Mackin, *Divorce and Remarriage,* p. 279.

developed in the East to care for matrimonial cases. With the breakdown of civil government in the West, however, bishops took over functions of government in all aspects of civil life, including marriage.

In the East, the emperor was the strong central authority who maintained Basil's benign teaching. Not only was the emperor himself married, but he was the protector of a church that cherished its priests' right to be married. In the West, celibacy was imposed on all clergy in major orders by an increasingly centralized papacy under Gregory VII.

So a strong impulse to legalize and centralize the administration of the discipline of marriage came from a papacy also committed to celibacy for the clergy, just when Augustine's teaching on divorce and remarriage was in the ascendancy.[26] Its implementation began with the decretals of Alexander III (1159–1181), the first canon lawyer to become pope. The present teaching of the Western church on absolute indissolubility was established. Subsequent events will show this to be one of those teachings of which Rahner said: "Although they can make no claim to be definitive, [they] are nonetheless presented in such a way as though in fact they are definitive."[27]

Notwithstanding the absolute position in the West, neither the Council of Florence (1438–1445?) nor the Council of Trent (1545–1563) challenged the Eastern practice. The Council of Florence sought to promote reunion with the Greeks. From April 1438 to July 1439, every issue thought to be seriously divisive between the Eastern and Western churches was studied in great detail. The Eastern practice of allowing remarriage after divorce was not brought up in those discussions. Only eight days after solemn promulgation of the agreement between the two churches did the pope raise a question about divorce practice among the Greeks. The Greeks' only reply was that it was not allowed without reason.[28] Clearly the practice on divorce was not a serious issue on which the Latin church could not yield.

Over a century later the Council of Trent came close, without

---

[26]Brundage, *Law, Sex and Christian Society in Medieval Europe*, p. 183.

[27]Karl Rahner, "Open Questions in Dogma Considered by the Institutional Church as Definitively Answered," *Journal of Ecumenical Studies*, vol. 15, no. 2 (Spring 1978), p. 212.

[28]Joseph Gill, S.J., *The Council of Florence* (Cambridge: University Press, 1959), pp. 296–297.

mentioning the Greeks by name, to condemning their practice on divorce and remarriage. At the last minute, at the urging of the Republic of Venice with its large Greek population, the council fathers drew back.

> Tradition on this point was not absolutely clear. Above all it was desired not to offend the non-united Greeks who allowed remarriage in such cases. The wording is thus carefully designed so that it only demands acceptance of the Latin standpoint without expressly condemning the other.[29]

Although Pius XI stated in *Casti connubii* that the Latin church's teaching was binding on the universal church, we will see from interventions at Vatican Council II and the 1980 Synod of Bishops that discussion is not closed.

Call for Change

In spite of widespread severity of the divorce problem, there was practically no evidence of pastoral concern about the issue at Vatican II. The final documents contained only one reference "to the plague of divorce" (*Gaudium et spes,* no. 47) and a statement that authentic conjugal love "will never be profaned by adultery or divorce" (no. 49).

One prophetic intervention, however, addressed the issue. Archbishop Elie Zoghbi, Melkite-rite patriarchal vicar in Egypt, asked if the church could not dispense the innocent party in a broken marriage from the matrimonial bond as was done in some Eastern churches?

> The counsel to live a life of solitude and continence is not for everyone because it calls for heroic virtue which cannot be imposed indiscriminately. Could not the Church, without prejudice to her doctrine on the indissolubility of marriage, use her authority on behalf of the innocent party in these cases as has been the case in the Christian Orient? This practice was also followed sometimes in the West.

---

[29] Josef Neuner, S.J., and Heinrich Roos, S.J., *The Teaching of the Catholic Church: As Contained in Her Documents,* ed. Karl Rahner, S.J. (Staten Island: Alba House, 1967), p. 355.

Zoghbi called attention to the care exercised at Trent in its choice of a formula that would not offend the Orthodox.

Cardinal Charles Journet challenged Zoghbi. He insisted that divorce had only entered the Eastern church through adoption of the law of Justinian, thus following a human policy rather than the gospel.

Zoghbi replied that

> the Justinian Code, promulgated toward the middle of the sixth century and adopting Eastern discipline on marriage, could not in any way have influenced Origen, St. Basil, St. John Chrysostom and others who lived during a period ranging between 300 and 150 years before this code, which merely recorded the previous teaching and practice of the Churches of the East.[30]

Furthermore, he noted, this teaching went back long before separation between East and West and had never been challenged in councils in which Eastern and Western bishops sat together.

Journet's effort was a rather crude example of a tendency we have already seen to make ancient evidence fit the Latin church's present teaching and practice.

By the time of the 1980 Synod of Bishops, the problem of divorced and remarried Catholics had become a principal concern of bishops from every part of the world.[31] Western and non-Western members of the synod alike raised concern for the innocent party in divorces and for the problem of stable second marriages involved in bringing up children.

Archbishop Derek Worlock (Liverpool) brought results of a presynodal consultation with priests and people of his diocese. He said that the "synod must listen to this voice of experienced priests and laity pleading for consideration of this problem of their less happy brethren,... spiritually destitute" though not physically starving. He spoke of

---

[30] *Council Daybook,* 138th General Congregation, September 29, 1965 (Washington, D.C.: National Catholic Welfare Conference, 1965), p. 69.

[31] Jan Grootaers and Joseph A. Selling, *The 1980 Synod of Bishops "On the Role of the Family": Exposition of the Event and an Analysis of Its Texts,* Bibliotheca Ephemeridum Theologicarum Lovaniensium (Leuven: Leuven University Press, 1983), p. 100.

Catholics whose first marriages have perished and who have now a second and more stable (if legally only civil) union in which they seek to bring up a new family. Often such persons, especially in their desire to help their children, long for restoration of full eucharistic communion with the church and its Lord. Is this spirit of repentance and desire for sacramental strength to be forever frustrated? Can they be told only that they must reject their new responsibilities as a necessary condition of forgiveness and restoration to sacramental life?[32]

Particularly significant was the appeal from every side for study of the centuries' old recognition of the validity of second, non-sacramental marriages by the Orthodox. Typical was the statement of Patriarch Maximos V Hakimof of Antioch, referring to the Eastern church's very ancient practice as a solution in the present crisis. He said:

The Fathers of the Church at that time accepted that the divorced-remarried could again be admitted to the eucharist. On the basis of the principle of "Oeconomia," often invoked and applied in the East, the Synod would be in a position to approach this question and find a practical solution.[33]

Cardinal Basil Hume, speaking for the entire English-speaking group, called for objective norms for admission to the sacraments, based on study of the Eastern church's practice. Bishop Etchegaray, for the French-speaking, asked for a special commission to study Eastern practice. Proposition 14, submitted to the pope by all the bishops, even while excluding possibility of remarriage after divorce, called for study of the Eastern practice.

In his closing homily, John Paul accepted some of the recommendations in Proposition 14 that stressed pastoral care of the divorced and remarried. He then reaffirmed traditional norms under which they could be allowed to return to sacramental penance and communion — if they live together as "brother and

---

[32] *Origins,* vol. 10, no. 18 (October 9, 1980), p. 275.

[33] Grootaers and Selling, *The 1980 Synod of Bishops "On the Role of the Family,"* p. 101.

sister" in complete abstinence under circumstances in which no scandal is given by their receiving the sacraments.

The pope also effectively ruled out a type of internal forum solution widely recommended by many priests for those involved in hardship cases. This solution suggested that those who in sincere conscience were convinced that their former marriage was truly dead and that their present marriage was right before God could receive the Eucharist.

The pope departed from Proposition 14 in two ways. He forbade

> any pastor for whatever reason or pretext even of a pastoral nature to perform ceremonies of any kind for divorced people who remarry. Such ceremonies would give the impression of the celebration of a new, sacramentally valid marriage and would thus lead people into error concerning the indissolubility of a validly contracted marriage.[34]

Thus he ruled out a kind of ceremony recommended by theologians like Curran; while not church weddings, such celebrations bring a sense of blessing and support to those attempting to rebuild their lives.

But most significantly, John Paul completely left out any reference to Proposition 14f, where the bishops asked for a "new and extensive" study of practices of the Eastern churches. The pope closed the issue; he left no room for further study or pastoral adaptation.

Rights Denied

After arguments from scripture and tradition, the strongest remaining argument against relaxing present discipline is that to do so would open the floodgates of divorce and promote further deterioration in family stability. But Catholic divorce rates in this country are now the same as those of Protestants and Jews not under such a strict discipline.[35] Maintenance of rigid discipline has not prevented the increase of divorce among Catholics.

---

[34]Ibid., p. 330.
[35]Andrew M. Greeley, *American Catholics Since the Council: An Unauthorized Report* (Chicago: Thomas More, 1985), pp. 15–16.

Lay reaction suggests that, among the People of God, the official position is not accepted as the final, irrevocable answer. The *New York Times*/CBS News poll of August 24, 1986, shows that 73 percent of American Catholics disagree with the official teaching and believe that they can hold such an opinion and remain good Catholics. This cannot be due to rationalization on the part of those who need to justify their disobedient conduct, since only about 26 percent of the Catholics in this country have been divorced at least once.

It is often argued that scandal will be given by a relaxation of current practice. If available statistics are any indication, lack of compassion toward people in great suffering and need gives even greater scandal. It is a question of who is being scandalized. Should our concern be only for those who will not accept change in church teaching? What of the scandal of those who ask: Is it moral in the face of so much suffering by so many millions of the church's own members to maintain a discipline with such a weak biblical, historical, and doctrinal foundation?

The right to marry is a fundamental, if sometimes limited, human right. Is it moral to deny the possibility of remarriage to those whose first marriages have irreparably ended? The right to the Eucharist is a fundamental right of the baptized, not a privilege granted by the hierarchy, but a gift offered to his own by the Lord of the church. Grave questions arise about an authority that affirms indissolubility as an "essential"[36] property of marriage and yet dissolves "indissoluble" marriages while claiming that it cannot dissolve the consummated marriages of baptized Christians. There is adequate historical basis for a "probable" opinion that the church can dissolve these marriages as well.

---

[36] 1983 Code of Canon Law, canon 1056.

Chapter 8

Democracy in the Church: The Election of Bishops

Democracy is the worst form of government except all those other forms
that have been tried from time to time.

— *Winston Churchill*

Preceding chapters have explored two areas where Roman Catholic teaching and discipline have caused suffering and estrangement for many Catholics and are obstacles to reunion with other Christian churches. In each case I have shown that Catholics — faced with a rigid and authoritarian magisterium — have resources from our oldest tradition that allow freedom in decision making and are helpful for dialogue.

But a question arises: Does failure to respond to such important needs in these and other areas indicate a flaw in the church's contemporary institutional structure?

Compare the case of *Humanae vitae* with reception of Gentiles into the early church. Before *Humanae vitae*'s promulgation, a crisis had developed among devout, married laity because official teaching on contraception no longer corresponded to their experience. A growing number of highly respected theologians reached the conclusion that the teaching could and should be changed. John XXIII established a commission on birth control but died before anything could be accomplished. Three cardinals and a patriarch raised the issue at Vatican II's fourth session. By their applause, the assembled bishops made it clear that they wanted it discussed. Paul VI, however, removed the issue from the council.

Pope Paul enlarged John's commission and stacked it in favor of traditional teaching. After careful study, the commission voted overwhelmingly for change. Fourteen cardinals and bishops were added to the last session, bringing the total number appointed to sixteen. Why were they added? To turn the com-

117

mission around. But of the sixteen, one appointee did not attend
and only three voted to keep the old teaching.

Humanae vitae has not been accepted in the church and, at
the 1980 Synod, the bishops were rebuffed in their effort to re-
open the case. John Paul II continues to demand the encyclical's
acceptance and insists that the issue is not open for discussion
by theologians.

Contrast the handling of this crisis with the early church's
treatment of the reception of Gentiles. Although thousands of
Jews had been received into the young church through baptism
(Acts 2:41), the possibility of receiving uncircumcised Gentiles
seemed so unlikely that Peter had to be prepared for this drastic act by a special vision (Acts 10:9–16). Moreover, the Holy
Spirit fell on the household of the Gentile Cornelius before Peter
decided to accept them (Acts 10:44–48).

Peter was called upon to explain his action, and the question
was raised again later when Paul and Barnabas also accepted
Gentiles. In Luke's account of the settlement of the issue at the
so-called Council of Jerusalem, James, not one of the Twelve
but the "brother of the Lord,"[1] presided (Acts 15:13–21) and
decisions were made by "the apostles and the elders, with the
whole church" (Acts 15:22).

The Vatican's handling of the birth control issue resembled
the decision making of a divine-right monarch; the Council of
Jerusalem resembled a New England town meeting.

Certainly, an international institution like the Roman Catholic church cannot operate like a town meeting. As the church has
grown in size and responsibilities, necessary changes in structure
have occurred. New structures, however, must be faithful to fundamental gospel values and sensitive to the special needs of the
contemporary situation. The church needs structures more re-
sponsive to the Spirit's voice at work among the people of God.
I believe that democracy, with its openness and accountability,
would be as fair and effective in the church as it has been in
secular government.

In what follows, I will show what I mean by democracy in
the church and explore evidence for democracy in the church's
history, emphasizing the ancient practice of popular election of

---

[1] For the question of the identity of James, see *Jerome Biblical Commentary*
(Englewood Cliffs, N.J.: Prentice-Hall, 1968), p. 796.

bishops. We will then see how the people's right to elect their bishops was lost, first to the clergy, then to secular rulers. In the Investiture Struggle, from 1050 to 1300, the church won back control over election of bishops from secular rulers only to have it become, at least in appearance, the preserve of cathedral chapters. Today, the papacy has taken over episcopal appointments.

The centuries have seen development of strong centralization in the church. Before the eleventh century, the church was a collegial group of local churches making up the universal church. But during the long Investiture Struggle between popes and secular rulers for control over Western Europe, popes, though unable to gain control over the empire and secular states, centralized control over the church, giving it the authoritarian character it has maintained to our day.

In the next chapter I will describe this struggle and present Brian Tierney's thesis that from writings of great church lawyers at the time of that struggle came constitutional principles and structures that characterize modern democracy. With Tierney, I propose that these principles and structures, developed within the church's own tradition, should be adopted by the modern church.

What Is Democracy?

To call the church a democracy is not to say that the church has been established by a contract among its members. No, the church is God's con-*gre*-gation, that is, the *grex,* the flock, that God has gathered together. The church is God's con-*voca*-tion, that is, the people God has *called* together.

Since God does not govern the church directly, however, but through human beings, it is both legitimate and necessary to ask what type of government comes closest to realizing the New Testament ideal. I doubt that autocracy, in which the educated, privileged few teach and control the uneducated masses, the so-called simple faithful, ever realized that ideal. Autocracy is particularly inappropriate in the modern world. The form of church government that accords best with the gospel spirit is democracy.

When we speak of democracy it is not necessary to intend the particular institutional structures set forth in the U.S. Constitution. Great Britain, the Netherlands, and the Scandinavian countries show that monarchical structures are compatible with genuine democracy. Opposition is not between democracy and monarchy, but between democracy and autocracy.

Brian Tierney's description of "constitutionalism" includes elements that are important in any discussion of democracy in the church.[2] Constitutionalism involves such basic ideas as "government under law" or "government by consent." It means guarantee of due process of law, where the law itself does not depend on an autocratic ruler's arbitrary will, but reflects the entire society's moral principles. It does not mean that a majority can force its will on a minority. Rather it means that machinery exists to develop a consensus that all citizens can be persuaded to accept, even if sometimes without enthusiasm. Characteristically this involves an elected representative assembly that makes laws and imposes taxes.

Such a system is usually called "constitutional democracy." To call it "participatory democracy" brings out even more clearly its importance for the realization of fundamental human values. In a chapter entitled "Intersubjectivity by Participation," Karol Wojtyla (nine years before his election as Pope John Paul II) wrote of the importance of participation.[3] Wojtyla said that by participation, by "acting with others," the human person, as an individual, realizes personal transcendence and integration. Moreover, "any authentic human community" is founded also on participation. He wrote of these two aspects of participation:

> The human community is strictly related to the experience of the person. . . . We find in it the reality of participation as that essential of the person which enables him to exist and act "together with others" and thus to reach his own fulfillment. Simultaneously, participation as an essential of the person is a constitutive factor of any human community.

Wojtyla proposed two "authentic" attitudes for community: solidarity and opposition.

---

[2]Brian Tierney, "Medieval Canon Law and Western Constitutionalism," *Catholic Historical Review,* 52 (1966), pp. 2–3, reprinted in *Church Law and Constitutional Thought in the Middle Ages* (London: Variorum Reprints, 1979), no. 15.

[3]Karol Wojtyla, *The Acting Person,* trans. Andrezej Potocki (Boston: D. Reidel, 1979), pp. 261–300.

The attitude of solidarity is, so to speak, the natural conse-
quence of the fact that human beings live and act together;
it is the attitude of a community, in which the common
good properly conditions and initiates participation, and
participation in turn properly serves the common good.

Of "the attitude of opposition," Wojtyla wrote:

Opposition is not inconsistent with solidarity.... Far from
rejecting the common good or the need of participation,
it consists on the contrary in their confirmation.... Those
who in this way stand up in opposition do not thereby
cut themselves off from their community. On the contrary,
they seek their own place and a constructive role within
the community....

In fact, society should be so structured that opposition can be
expressed and operate in the society for the society's good. He
continued:

More precisely, in order for opposition to be constructive,
the structure, and beyond it the system of communities of
a given society must be such as to allow the opposition
that emerges from the soil of solidarity not only to *express*
itself within the framework of the given community but
also to *operate* for its benefit. The structure of a human
community is correct only if it admits not just the presence
of a justified opposition but also that practical effectiveness
of opposition required by the common good and the right
of participation.

Wojtyla then describes what he calls "a sense of dialogue."

The common good has to be conceived of dynamically and
not statically.... In fact, it must liberate and support the
attitude of solidarity but never to a degree such as to stifle
opposition.... The principle of dialogue allows us to select
and bring to light what in controversial situations is right
and true, and helps to eliminate any partial, preconceived
or subjective views and trends.

To these ideas on constitutionalism and participation, I would add from Catholic social thought the important principle of subsidiarity, which protects individual rights and prevents the absorption of smaller units of society by a monopolizing, central power. Subsidiarity safeguards freedom of action and participation throughout the various levels of society. Pius XI wrote in *Quadragesimo anno*:

> Just as it is gravely wrong to take from individuals what they can accomplish by their own initiative and industry and give it to the community, so also it is an injustice and at the same time a great evil and disturbance of right order to assign to a greater and higher association what lesser and subordinate organizations can do. For every social activity ought of its very nature furnish help to the members of the body social and never absorb them.[4]

In preparation for the 1985 extraordinary synod, almost all bishops' conferences referred explicitly or equivalently to the principle of subsidiarity. Cardinal Hamer, however, apparently speaking for the curia, rejected application of the principle of subsidiarity to the church because of its sociopolitical connotations.[5]

I propose that principles of constitutional or participatory democracy and subsidiarity apply to the church. The church is a voluntary society,[6] established by God, though never directly governed by God, only by human agency. All norms recognized as essential to good governance and authentic community in civil society apply equally to the church.

Roots of Church Democracy

Democratic structures already exist in the Roman Catholic church. The Second Vatican Council exemplified democracy

---

[4] *AAS* 23:203; 79.

[5] Patrick Granfield, *The Limits of the Papacy: Authority and Autonomy in the Church* (New York: Crossroad, 1987), pp. 125–132.

[6] "Voluntary" in the sociological sense. Juridically, incorporation into the church is through baptism, and an older theology denied the possibility of leaving. See James H. Provost, "The People of God," book 2, part 1, in *The Code of Canon Law: A Text and Commentary,* ed. James A. Coriden et al. (New York: Paulist, 1985), pp. 119–129, esp. p. 129, "Leaving the Church."

in action. Opinion had been widespread that, with the definition of papal infallibility, councils would no longer be needed or held. After Vatican I, it seemed the pope would function as the church's sole teacher. Vatican II, however, showed what could be accomplished in the church when all the bishops worked together, with significant input from theologians (some formerly silenced) and Protestant observers. Above all, because of the press, input came from the church at large. The press kept the laity informed and the laity made their concerns known to the bishops.

The wider church's importance is evident in actions and themes of the council. A significant action was the reversal of the order of the second and third chapters of *Lumen gentium,* when the original schema, with its emphasis on the church as hierarchy, was altered. The council fathers deliberately placed the chapter on the church as the "People of God" ahead of a chapter on the church's hierarchical structure.

The council acknowledged the importance of the "sense of the faithful," *sensus fidelium.* It also taught that infallibility of pope and bishops has meaning only in the context of the fundamental infallibility of the church as a whole.

These democratic tendencies at Vatican II have deep roots, going back to the New Testament church with its community participation and absence of authoritarian structures. Even the Twelve were not part of a continuing structural element in the future church.[7] So uncertain are structures in the New Testament period that it is not possible to distinguish between presbyters and bishops, but more accurate to speak of presbyter-bishops. It is true that Paul, according to Acts 14:23, appointed elders in churches he founded. But the rest of the New Testament evidence about choosing leaders and about decision making — election of Matthias (Acts 1:12–26), election of the seven (Acts 6:1–6), and events that Luke described at the "Council of Jerusalem" (Acts 15) — points to a high level of involvement by the whole community.

---

[7] Raymond E. Brown, S.S., *Priest and Bishop: Biblical Reflections* (New York: Paulist, 1970), p. 55. The Twelve had no successors. Their function was to symbolize the continuity between the twelve tribes of Israel and the church and to act as the witnesses to the earthly life of Jesus and to his resurrection (Acts 1:21–22).

Of the Council of Jerusalem, Myles Bourke writes that, although leaders' roles were important, it is clear that the entire community took part in the discussion.[8] He concluded that any church assembly not involving the laity in an active role does not meet standards set by Luke in his description of the Jerusalem council.

Further, Bourke suggests the importance in decision making of teachers (*didaskaloi*), ranked third by Paul, after apostles and prophets (1 Cor. 12:28). Bourke identifies them with theologians in the present church, and comments that, if the "whole church" is to have a role, particularly in the making of decisions in matters of faith, then the authority of theologians should be given much greater weight than is often the case today.

After surveying all relevant biblical texts, Patrick Granfield of Catholic University concludes that two important democratic goals, majoritarian principles and decentralization, were operative in the New Testament church's decision making. He notes especially absence of authoritarianism and the open atmosphere that promoted free discussion of issues crucial to the community. New Testament evidence, therefore, would suggest that the laity should have an active role in every church assembly when matters that concern them are discussed.

A monarchical church structure, so easily but mistakenly considered anti-democratic, seems to have developed in the churches of Asia Minor around A.D. 100.[9] For centuries, Ignatius's description of local church structure, a bishop surrounded by his presbyters and deacons, was thought to be normative for the entire early second-century church.

But for some years now, it has been recognized that, at least in Rome, this was not the earliest structure. Evidence in the letters of Ignatius and the *Shepherd of Hermas* would indicate that the Roman church was governed by a small group of presbyter-bishops. A monarchical structure, evident from the writings of Ignatius in the churches of Asia Minor, does not seem to have developed in Rome until mid-second century.[10]

---

[8] Myles M. Bourke, "Collegial Decision-Making in the New Testament," *The Jurist: Studies in Co-Responsibility,* vol. 31, no. 1 (1971), pp. 4–13. Bourke is a former president of the Catholic Biblical Association.

[9] Raymond E. Brown, S.S., and John P. Meier, *Antioch and Rome: New Testament Cradles of Catholic Christianity* (New York: Paulist, 1983), p. 77.

[10] Moreover, a commonly held view that Peter was bishop in Rome is not

Witnesses of the earliest period point to variety rather than uniformity.[11]

The People's Bishops

A review of the first centuries reveals important democratic elements in the life of the early church.[12] In the third century in the West, not only did the people elect their bishops, but it was considered important that they do so. The *Apostolic Tradition* of Hippolytus from around 230 stated:

> Let the bishop be ordained after he has been chosen by all the people. When he has been named and shall please all, let him, with the presbytery and such bishops as may be present, assemble with the people on a Sunday. While all give their consent, the bishops shall lay their hands upon him, and the presbyters shall stand by in silence.[13]

Cyprian of Carthage, writing to an African council in Spain in 254, warned the people to separate themselves from a sinful leader,

> especially since they themselves have the power either of electing worthy bishops or of rejecting the unworthy. We see that this very fact also comes from divine authority that a bishop be chosen in the presence of the people before the eyes of all and that he be approved as worthy and fit by public judgment and testimony.[14]

---

supported by the evidence. See John Fuellenbach, S.V.D., *Ecclesiastical Office and the Primacy of Rome: An Evaluation of Recent Theological Discussion of First Clement* (Washington: Catholic University of America Press, 1980), p. 116.

[11]John E. Lynch, "Co-responsibility in the First Five Centuries: Presbyteral Colleges and the Election of Bishops," *The Jurist: Studies in Co-responsibility,* vol. 31, no. 1 (1971), pp. 18–21.

[12]See William W. Bassett, ed., *The Choosing of Bishops: Historical and Theological Studies* (Hartford: Canon Law Society of America, 1971).

[13]*The Apostolic Tradition of Hippolytus,* trans. and ed. Burton Scott Easton (Hamden, Conn.: Archon Books, 1962), p. 33.

[14]*Letter* 67:3–4, *CSEL,* 3:737–738; *St. Cyprian: Letters (1–81),* trans. Sister Rose Bernard Donna, in *The Fathers of the Church,* 51 (Washington, D.C.: Catholic University Press, 1964), p. 234.

About the same time, Cyprian showed his concern for shared responsibility. In a letter to his priests and deacons, he wrote:

> From the beginning of my episcopate I decided to do nothing of my own opinion privately without your advice and the consent of the people.[15]

In Cyprian's election the people had prevailed against the local clergy. In the case of Martin of Tours in 371, they prevailed over neighboring bishops.[16]

In the election of Ambrose in Milan in the fourth century, the people gathered in the cathedral to choose a new bishop. Feelings ran high between Arian heretics, who had controlled the bishopric, and Catholics, who hoped to gain control. A catechumen at the time, Ambrose, as governor of the province, went to the church to prevent a disturbance. When he spoke soothing words, a voice (said to have been that of a child) called out: "Ambrose for bishop!" The whole congregation, Arians and Catholics alike, took up the cry. Ambrose made serious attempts to avoid the office, but was finally baptized. He passed through the various grades of the ministry in six days and was consecrated bishop on December 1 in 373.

Dudden observes that although the people's choice was approved by a majority of the clergy, the chief factor in Ambrose's election was the call by the people. It was the Western custom, he claims, that the people elected, the clergy concurred, and the neighboring bishops examined, approved, and consecrated. If the parties were divided, the people's will usually prevailed. Dudden's description may oversimplify a complicated pattern. Nevertheless, the influence of the people was normally significant.

An excellent example of respect for local sensibilities and autonomy can be seen in a letter of Pope Julius (337–352). Athanasius had been arbitrarily replaced in the see of Alexandria by one Gregory. Julius wrote:

---

[15] *Letter* 14:4, *CSEL,* 3, 2:512; ibid., p. 43.
[16] F. Homes Dudden, *The Life and Times of St. Ambrose,* vol. 1 (Oxford: Clarendon Press, 1935), pp. 70–71. For a thorough discussion of the sometimes conflicting evidence see Lynch, "Co-responsibility in the First Five Centuries," pp. 36–80.

For what canon of the Church, or what Apostolical tradition warrants this, that when a Church is at peace . . . Gregory should be sent thither, a stranger to the city, not having been baptized there, not known to the general body, and desired neither by Presbyters, nor Bishops, nor Laity?[17]

Subordination of the Laity

But a tendency to subordinate the laity's role to that of the clergy had already begun. In its fourth canon, the Council of Nicaea (325) provided that new bishops be appointed by all bishops of the province with confirmation by the metropolitan, that is, by the archbishop, the bishop who had the rank of primate in the province. This was repeated by the Councils of Antioch (341), Sardica (343), and Laodicea (c. 360), with the provision that the synod of bishops must be present at episcopal elections.

Pope Siricius (384–399), however, still spoke of presbyters and bishops being elected and chosen by the clergy and people.[18] He insisted only that there be no election in rural Italy "without knowledge of the Apostolic See."[19]

By the fifth century, provincial bishops had primary responsibility in election of new bishops. But consent of other groups remained a factor. Celestine I (422–432) wrote:

A bishop should not be given to those who are unwilling [to receive him]. The consent and the wishes of the clergy, the people, and the nobility are required.[20]

The frequently quoted statement of Pope Leo I (440–461) was simply: "He who governs all should be elected [*eligatur*] by all."[21] But in a letter written probably a year or so before, Leo seemed to distinguish between "election" by the clergy and the people's "request":

---

[17]*Apologia contra Arianos*, 30; *PG* 25:297.

[18]Siricius, *Letter* 1:10, *PL* 13:1143.

[19]*Letter* 5.2.1, *PL* 13:1157A.

[20]*Letter* 4:5, *PL* 50:434. See Robert L. Benson, *The Bishop-elect: A Study in Medieval Ecclesiastical Office* (Princeton: Princeton University Press, 1968), pp. 24–25.

[21]*Letter* 10:6, *PL* 54:634.

It would be unreasonable to count among the bishops those who were not elected [*electi*] by the clergy, requested [*expetiti*] by the people, or consecrated by the bishops of the province with the approval of the metropolitan.[22]

In 446, Leo gave a practical reason for the people's approval:

No one, of course, is to be consecrated against the wishes of the people and without their requesting [*petentibus*] it. Otherwise, the citizens will despise or hate the bishop they do not want and thus become less religious than they should, on the grounds that they were not permitted to have a man of their choice.[23]

As Robert L. Benson, a historian who specializes in the medieval period, points out, in the fifth century *electi* could mean elect in a narrow sense, but it could be used in a non-technical sense to signify choice, preference, or approval. Leo himself could speak at one time of "election" (*eligatur*) by clergy and laity alike, at another of the clergy's "election" (*electi sunt*) and people's "request" (*expetiti*). In practice as well as in theory, the fifth-century papacy generally distinguished differing parts played by clergy and laity, assigning higher status to clerical "election."[24]

Meaningful election by those to be governed continued in the church a century later in the Rule of St. Benedict (529) with its provision for the abbot's election by the monastic community.[25] Moreover, democracy in the monastery did not end with election. Benedict provided for a high level of consultation by the abbot. For lesser matters, he was to consult a council of seniors. For more important matters, the whole community was to be consulted. Benedict also insisted that age should not be prejudicial to order in the community: "Remember that Samuel and

---

[22] *Letter* 167, *PL* 45:1203.

[23] *Letter* 14:5, *PL* 54:673.

[24] Robert L. Benson, "Reflections on Co-responsibility in the Historical Church," *The Jurist: Studies in Co-responsibility,* vol. 31, no. 1 (1971), p. 58.

[25] *The Rule of St. Benedict in Latin and English with Notes* (Collegeville, Minn.: Liturgical Press, 1981), ch. 64. The Rule speaks of "the one selected either by the whole community acting unanimously in the fear of God, or by some part of the community, no matter how small, which possesses sounder judgment" (65:1). For the various interpretations see pp. 372–375.

factions of the Roman nobility and interference by Holy Roman emperors, had devastating consequences. In the century and a half before the beginning of reform under Pope Leo IX (1048–1054), there were thirty-six popes, compared to eleven in the last 150 years in our own time.

Beginning early in the tenth century, one woman, Marozia, and her son, Alberic II, dominated the papacy for thirty-six years. According to the *Liber pontificalis,* Marozia was Pope Sergius III's mistress. She controlled selection of popes from 928 to 932. One of her appointees was her twenty-nine-year-old son, probably by Sergius, who became Pope John XI. From 936 to his death in 954, Alberic II controlled the papacy. Before his death he arranged for his illegitimate son to become Pope John XII (d. 964).

With John XII, control of the papacy shifted to the Holy Roman emperors. In 962, Pope John XII crowned Otto I emperor. Otto promised John temporal control over almost three-fourths of Italy. In exchange, Otto made John recognize imperial suzerainty over the papal states and made him agree that future popes could not be consecrated until they had taken an oath of fealty to the emperor as their overlords. John's subsequent revolt against imperial control was unsuccessful.

Except for a short period from 1003 to 1012, emperors controlled the election of popes until the electoral reform of Nicholas II in 1059. The popes crowned the emperors and the emperors appointed the popes. Approval of the imperial court was sought in every papal election until that of Stephen XI in 1057. Even St. Leo IX, under whom the Gregorian reform began, was appointed pope in 1048 by his cousin, Emperor Henry III. The 1059 electoral decree finally limited papal elections to the college of cardinals, pastors of the principal, or cardinal (from *cardo,* hinge), churches of the city of Rome. Until this day, at least nominally, the cardinals still hold the title of pastors of parish churches in Rome.

Clerical Control Regained

One of the great, but short-lived, triumphs of the Gregorian reform was the restoration of the ancient ideal of election of bishops by clergy and people. At the beginning of reform under Leo IX, the Synod of Reims (1049) decreed: "Without the elec-

Daniel were still boys when they judged their elders (1 Sa
Dan. 13:44–62)."

It is true that, according to the Rule, the abbot, after liste
to all, makes final decisions. To my observation that Bene
still felt the influence of the autocratic forms of civil gov
ment of his day, one wise student of the Rule suggested that
abbot's role in making the final decision should not be seer
an exercise of autocratic power, but rather as implementir
consensus.

Secular Control

The people's loss of involvement coincided with the fall of
Roman Empire, usually dated 476, and the political collap
of civilization in the West. Struggles between military factio
widespread disease and famine, and serious impoverishment
the preceding century left the empire powerless before invadir
Germanic tribes. Western Europe underwent a period of stee
cultural decline, which lasted until around 1000.

The moral and educational decline of clergy and laity dur
ing the Germanic invasions and abuses in the election proces
in this period of turmoil led to the people's loss of the righ
to elect their bishops. With the breakdown of civil government, many bishops, the only educated and competent personnel available, became heavily involved in temporal administration. Under the feudal system, bishops were both secular and ecclesiastical rulers of their bishoprics, vassals of the
overlords of the area. As temporal rulers they were appointed
by king or emperor, who may have been laymen, but whose
choices scarcely considered the needs of the people or of the
church.

Before the beginning of the Gregorian reform, monarchs normally appointed bishops and "invested" them with ring and
crosier, symbols of their office. This gave enormous control over
church affairs to the rulers who chose the bishops and to bishops
who were usually not selected because of their religious qualifications.

The drastic need for reform can be seen in the church in
Rome. The bishop of Rome, who by his election automatically
became pope, was, at least theoretically, elected by the clergy
and people of the city. Serious abuses, involving contending

tion of the clergy and the people, no one may be advanced to an ecclesiastical office."[26]

In his attack on lay investiture, however, Cardinal Humbert (1054–1058) prepared for reduction of the people's role. He insisted that:

> According to the decrees of the holy fathers anyone who is consecrated as a bishop is first elected by the clergy, then requested by the people, and finally consecrated by the bishops of the province with the approval of the metropolitan.[27]

The issue was far from settled. At the beginning of the next century, in his *Tractatus de regia potestate* (1102–1104), Hugh of Fleury could say "that a king, inspired by the Holy Spirit, can appoint a pious cleric to the honor of prelacy." But, he continued:

> If, indeed, a bishop has been elected by clergy and people reasonably and according to ecclesiastical custom the king ought not to use force against the electors tyrannically or harass them but should lawfully give his consent to the ordination.

The popes' struggle to take control of episcopal appointments from emperors lasted half a century. It ended with a compromise in the Concordat of Worms (1122). The emperor could no longer appoint bishops and abbots. They had to be canonically elected in the emperor's presence. Only after election did the emperor bestow the temporalities for which the bishop was to "perform his lawful duties" as the emperor's vassal.

The early period saw great variety in the composition of assemblies gathered to elect bishops. For an election in Angers in 1102, the summons included "neighboring bishops and abbots and religious men."[28] A high point in the restoration of the ancient ideal came in canon 28 of the Second Lateran Council in

---

[26]Benson, "Reflections on Co-responsibility in the Historical Church," p. 59.

[27]Brian Tierney, *The Crisis of Church & State 1050–1300* (Englewood Cliffs, N.J.: Prentice-Hall, 1964), p. 40.

[28]Benson, "Reflections on Co-responsibility in the Historical Church," p. 62.

1139. After anathematizing those who would leave a see vacant more than three months, the council continued:

> We do not allow the canons of the episcopal see to exclude religious men [*religiosos viros*] from the election of bishops, but, with their counsel, an honest and suitable person is to be elected as bishop. But if the election shall have been celebrated, these same religious men [*ejusdem religiosis*] having been excluded, the very fact that it was done without their consent and participation shall make such an election null and void.[29]

The phrase "religious men" could refer to abbots and other priests who did not belong to the cathedral chapter, or, in this early period, it could also include lay nobles and important laymen. Only the lower levels of lay society seem always to have been excluded.[30]

The end of the people's role was in sight. Around 1140, Gratian's *Decretum* appeared.[31] In this influential collection of ideas, church laws, and church practices from a thousand years of the church's history, Gratian sought to reconcile contradictory evidence of the preceding centuries. On election of bishops, he wrote:

> It is commanded that the people be summoned not to perform the election, but rather to give consent to the election. For election... belongs to priests, and the duty of the faithful people is to consent humbly.[32]

This "humble consent" was to be manifested by a popular acclamation of the newly elected bishop.[33] Anyone who has attended the ordination of a bishop or priest since Vatican II may have taken part in this now optional, symbolic gesture by which the laity present show consent by their applause.

---

[29] Mansi, 21:534.

[30] Benson, "Reflections on Co-responsibility in the Historical Church," p. 63.

[31] Gratian is thought to have been a twelfth-century Camaldolese monk; almost nothing is known about him except that he produced his *Concord of Discordant Canons,* usually known as the *Decretum.*

[32] *Distinctio,* no. 63.

[33] Benson, *Bishop-elect: A Study in Medieval Ecclesiastical Office,* p. 29.

In fact, Gratian himself was not above manipulating evidence to fit his desired conclusion. Immediately after this *dictum,* he quoted a short form of the statement of Celestine I: "The consent and the wishes of the clergy, and the people, are required."[34] But Gratian introduced this quotation from Celestine with the rubric: "It is not for the people to elect, but to consent to the election." Celestine had used "consent" and "wishes" without distinction among clergy, people, and nobility. Gratian's rubric clearly implies that it is the laity who do the consenting after the clergy have done the electing.[35]

Gratian then quoted Leo's famous letter, but omitted the sentence: "He who governs all should be elected [*eligatur*] by all." Later, in this long *Distinctio,* Gratian concluded: "From the foregoing authorities it is clear to everyone that election belongs only to clerics."

In the 1170s, Pope Alexander III, still acknowledging that "the favor and consent of the prince should be requested," wrote:

Nevertheless laymen must not be admitted to an election. ...If, therefore, laymen wish to meddle in such matters, you should be mindful of that decree in which it is said, "The people should be taught, not obeyed." When they have been excluded, you should proceed in the election harmoniously and canonically.[36]

By 1180, Alexander made it quite clear that the right of election really belonged to the cathedral canons, a minority of whom could override a contrary vote by attending abbots and other priests.

Papal Domination

The canons' victory was short-lived. Roman participation in the process began and foreshadowed increased papal control over the episcopacy. Pope Gregory VII (1075–1083) added a new element which pointed to future papal dominance in the choice

---

[34]*D* 63:26.
[35]Called to my attention by Dr. Thomas Amos, Hill Monastic Manuscript Library, St. John's Abbey, Collegeville, Minn.
[36]Benson, "Reflections on Co-responsibility in the Historical Church," p. 71.

of bishops. As a substitute for the metropolitan's confirmation of an election, he offered an alternative of papal confirmation. In an invalid election, Gregory provided that an appointment would be made by the Roman pontiff or metropolitan.

In the twelfth century, a radical new interpretation of the effect of confirmation added a powerful tool to Rome's increasing control of the episcopacy. In the making of a bishop, there were essentially three stages: election, confirmation, and consecration. In the earlier period, consecration had been considered the source of all a bishop's powers; a bishop-elect could not function until he had been consecrated. The First Lateran Council in 1123 decreed that a bishop, canonically elected but not consecrated, could not alienate church property, and that an attempt to do so would be invalid.[37]

This understanding of a bishop-elect's powers changed because of the canonists' study of Nicholas II's decree on papal elections. That decree made it clear that if a newly elected pope were already a bishop before election, he would not have to await his formal installation; he could exercise all his powers as soon as he accepted the election. This suggested that a bishop's sacramental and jurisdictional, or administrative, powers were distinct. Sacramental power to ordain priests and consecrate other bishops clearly depended upon consecration. Master Rufinus noted, however, that one did not have to be ordained to perform acts of administration.

Stephen of Tournai concluded that "power of administration," or jurisdiction, did not derive from either election or consecration, but solely from confirmation of the election. This new interpretation seriously eroded the clergy's influence in the election process. This new understanding of confirmation reduced the clergy's role to little more than proposing a candidate for the metropolitan's approval. This strong centralizing movement increased a bishop's dependence on the metropolitan, whose power and influence were proportionately, though only temporarily, enhanced.

In the thirteenth century, popes moved in to control metropolitans. Canonists accepted a pyramidal model of the church. The church on earth was thought to mirror the heavenly ranks of spirits, with inferior spirits joyfully and humbly obeying higher

---

[37]Benson, *Bishop-elect: A Study in Medieval Ecclesiastical Office,* p. 41.

ranks. Canonists applied this same hierarchical arrangement to the church, with the pope at the apex of the pyramid. If metropolitans could control their suffragan bishops by confirmation, then popes could control metropolitans by confirmation. So the decretists held:

> Just as the consent of the archbishop is necessary in the confirmation of the bishop... in the same way the consent of the supreme pontiff is needed in the confirmation of the archbishop.[38]

Desire to increase power and centralize control, rather than financial gain, seems to have been the primary motive behind the twelfth-century introduction of papal confirmation. But in the following century, the large "voluntary" gift expected for confirmation of an *electus* became an important source of papal revenue and a heavy burden on newly elected bishops.

A man temperamentally and intellectually capable of taking advantage of the developing situation was elected pope at the beginning of the thirteenth century. Innocent III (1198–1216), often described as the greatest medieval pope, more than any other pope pushed papal monarchy toward absolutism.[39] Innocent saw control over resignation, deposition, and translation of bishops as the touchstone of papal supremacy. Until the end of the twelfth century, no consistent rules existed governing transfer of bishops from one see to another. Certainly it did not require papal approval and authorization. Innocent changed that. To do so, he used a commonly held idea of the time that bishops were married to their churches. On this basis, he claimed that as only God could break the bond of a marriage, so only God could dissolve the bond between the bishop and his church. But, according to Innocent, Christ had granted a special privilege to Peter and his successors to dissolve unconsummated lay marriages, and also marriages between bishops and their churches. So, only the pope could dissolve episcopal marriages and transfer bishops. In *Quanto personam* Innocent wrote:

---

[38] Ibid., pp. 378–379.

[39] Kenneth Pennington, *Pope and Bishops: The Papal Monarchy in the Twelfth and Thirteenth Centuries* (Philadelphia: University of Pennsylvania Press, 1984), p. 58.

God, not man, separates a bishop from his Church because
the Roman pontiff dissolves the bond between them by divine rather than by human authority, carefully considering
the need and usefulness of each translation. The pope has
this authority because he does not exercise the office of
man, but of the true God on earth.[40]

But had not power to loose and bind, given to Peter in Matthew 16:18, also been given to the other apostles in Matthew
18:18? Would not all bishops as successors of the other apostles
have the same authority as Peter's successor? Later upholders
of papal absolutism would justify their position by reference to
Christ's words to Peter in John 21:15–17, "Feed my sheep." Innocent, however, used John 1:42. There Christ said to Simon
only: "You shall be called Cephas." Medieval etymologists recognized that the Greek word "head" transliterated into Latin
cephale. This permitted them to interpret the Aramaic *cephas*
as "head," untroubled that in the Greek New Testament *cephas*
was translated as "rock." Innocent combined John 1:42, "head,"
with Matthew 16:18, "rock," to show that primacy in the church
had been granted to Peter. Papal authority was thus clearly set
apart from episcopal authority. Innocent III held that, as Peter's
successor, he was the head of the church. To him not just human
law but divine institution required that important cases in the
church be referred to the pope. As head the pope had "fullness
of power" (*plenitudinem potestatis*).

Control of benefices illustrated the extent to which Innocent
centralized power in the papal office. Benefices, endowed ecclesiastical offices conferred on clerics for their financial support,
were normally at the bishops' disposal, and in the medieval period were frequently bestowed on unworthy persons. By the end
of his pontificate, Innocent had established the pope's legal right
to bestow benefices in *any* church.

Pope Innocent IV (1243–1254) based the right to control
benefices explicitly on the "fullness of papal power." Earlier
canonists justified use of fullness of papal power only in ex-
traordinarily important matters; Innocent IV used it to justify
interference in relatively unimportant diocesan affairs. Papal
monarchical authority was significantly extended.

---

[40]Ibid., p. 16.

Resort to papal courts increased papal control. In the secular sphere, kings increased control over their realms and gained important sources of revenue by providing satisfactory justice in their courts.[41] For similar reasons, bishops, abbots, and other litigants showed themselves more than willing to appeal cases to papal courts.[42]

Confirming bishops, approving transfers to better sees, conferring benefices,[43] and offering justice in its courts, all became sources of revenue, which in itself enhanced papal prestige and power. Frequently the pope quashed an election and then immediately appointed the *electus,* from whom, of course, the usual "voluntary" gift was expected.[44]

In the centuries that followed, Catholic rulers regained much influence in episcopal appointment through right of patronage (*ius patronatus*). Beginning in the sixteenth century, for financial considerations Rome granted Catholic monarchs the right to appoint bishops to sees that had been reserved to Rome itself.[45] These arrangements continued through a series of concordats entered into at the beginning of the nineteenth century between Pius VII and various Catholic rulers.[46] When rulers in Protestant countries sought to control episcopal appointments, Rome agreed to accept recommendations by cathedral chapters. As late as 1829, popes appointed only a limited number of bishops outside the papal states. Two principal methods of choosing candidates for the episcopacy were election by cathedral chapters and royal or imperial patronage.

An unusual situation in the United States led to worldwide appointment of bishops by Rome. In missionary countries governed by Catholic Spain and Portugal, right of patronage re-

---

[41]Joseph R. Strayer, *On the Medieval Origins of the Modern State* (Princeton: Princeton University Press, 1970), pp. 28–33.

[42]Brian Tierney, "The Continuity of Papal Political Theory in the Thirteenth Century: Some Methodological Considerations," *Medieval Studies* (Toronto) 27 (1965), p. 245 (reprinted in *Church Law,* 5).

[43]William E. Lunt, *Papal Revenues in the Middle Ages,* vol. 1 (New York: Columbia University Press, 1934), pp. 81–91.

[44]Benson, *Bishop-elect: A Study in Medieval Ecclesiastical Office,* p. 381, n. 16.

[45]Hervé-Marie Legrand, "Theology and the Election of Bishops in the Early Church," in Giuseppe Alberigo and Anton Weiler, eds., *Election and Consensus in the Church,* Concilium 77 (New York: Herder and Herder, 1972). pp. 33–34.

[46]Robert Trisco, "The Variety of Procedures in Modern History," in Bassett, *The Choosing of Bishops,* pp. 33–34.

mained in force and missionary bishops were appointed by the crown. But the American colonies had been founded from Protestant England. Moreover, no cathedral chapters existed to elect bishops, and separation of church and state precluded any interference by the American government. The first bishop, John Carroll, had been elected by twenty-six active priests in the United States and Pius VI accepted their choice. Subsequently, Pius VII accepted five candidates "elected" by American priests and bishops but appointed four without any consultation in the United States, in one case after rejecting their choice. While the American church favored French bishops, Rome imposed Irish bishops on it.

In 1810, the American bishops requested that right of nomination of future bishops be granted to the archbishop of Baltimore and his suffragans. Their request was refused. A decision was made that American bishops could only recommend possible appointees, whom the pope could freely accept or reject. This procedure was adopted for the whole church.[47]

With the secularization of Catholic states in Europe in the twentieth century, the church recovered control over episcopal appointment in those countries. Instead of restoring the right of election to cathedral chapters, however, appointment was reserved to Rome.[48] The 1917 Code claimed that the bishop of Rome "freely appoints" the other bishops and that the right of any others to appoint is a concession.[49] At that time, only about half the world's bishops were appointed by Rome. Today, at least in the Latin rite, Roman control of episcopal appointments is almost complete.[50]

In the discussion on collegiality at Vatican II, Patriarch Maximos IV Saigh insisted that "appointment of bishops is not restricted by divine right to the Roman Pontiff." He urged that this merely historical development in the Western church should not be made a rule of law for the entire world.[51]

---

[47] Peter Hebblethwaite, *In the Vatican* (Bethesda, Md.: Adler & Adler, 1986), pp. 93–94.

[48] Hervé-Marie Legrand, "Theology and the Election of Bishops in the Early Church," p. 34.

[49] Canon 329, 2 and 3.

[50] For the exceptions, see Granfield, *The Limits of the Papacy,* pp. 75–76.

[51] Floyd Anderson, ed., *Council Daybook,* Vatican II, Session 1, Oct. 11 to Dec. 8, 1962–Session 2, Sept. 29 to Dec. 4, 1963 (Washington: National Catholic Welfare Conference, 1965), p. 168.

The 1983 Code ignored this call to broaden the method of choosing bishops. Canon 377, 1, states: "The Supreme Pontiff freely appoints bishops or confirms those who have been legitimately elected." Norms of the Code for selection of bishops are carefully devised to avoid even the appearance that those consulted have a right to elect. In the long and strictly secret process for obtaining names of suitable candidates for the episcopal office,

> the pontifical legate is to hear some members of the college of consultors, and of the Cathedral chapter, and *if he judges it expedient,* he shall also obtain, *individually and in secret,* the opinion of other members of the secular and religious clergy as well as of the laity who are outstanding for their wisdom.[52]

Clergy and laity, who *may,* but need not, be asked, are not to be consulted "collectively," lest it appear that they are involved in actually choosing their future bishops.

From Popular Election to Papal Appointment

It has been a long journey: from election of bishops by the people, to election by people and clergy, to election by clergy with the people's approval, to election by the synod of bishops with the metropolitan's approval, to loss of control to secular rulers, to control regained by the church with election by cathedral chapters, to control by the papacy in the thirteenth century through power to confirm. The long and involved story came to a climax with the claim of the 1917 Code of Canon Law that the bishop of Rome "freely appoints" other bishops and that the right of any others to appoint is a concession.

The original reasons for the people's election of their bishops remain valid. Leo the Great's assertion — "He who governs all should be elected by all" — still holds. Election of their bishops by clergy and people has deep roots in the communitarian, democratic nature of a church whose leaders are called to serve and not to be served.

---

[52]Canon 377, 3; emphasis added.

The popular election of bishops, with necessary procedural safeguards, is a development much to be desired and seriously needed. Only such a structural reform can counter damaging authoritarianism and lead to the rapport between the People of God and their leaders needed for the church and its mission.

Chapter 9

Democracy in the Church: The Struggle for Power

The kings of the Gentiles exercise lordship over them; and those in authority over them are called benefactors. But not so with you; rather let the greatest among you become as the youngest, and the leader as one who serves.

—Luke 22:25–26

In his column "Q.E.D." in *The Critic,* John L. McKenzie wrote: "The infallibility syndrome is a symptom, not a disease. The disease is the compulsion to impose doctrine upon the faithful, to control thinking and expression." Speaking of the Roman Curia he asked:

Yet it seeks to impose — what? Not faith and morals, certainly. What is sought is power; and the lust for power needs no explanation which would be different from an explanation elsewhere. It is pleasant to have power, and no one needs to explain why he wants it.[1]

In chapter 4, we considered Laeuchli's thesis that anti-sexual legislation at the Council of Elvira (c. 309) was part of a clerical effort to gain control over the laity. I have suggested that the same desire for power may have motivated retention of the prohibition of contraception and imposition of a rigid discipline on divorce and remarriage. We have also seen in our historical survey of episcopal elections that the people and clergy's power to choose, recovered from secular rulers during the Investiture Struggle, was not returned to the people and clergy, but became an important element in the centralization of power in the papacy. Before that conflict began, the church could have been

---

[1] *The Critic,* December 1968–January 1969, p. 94.

seen as a collegial group of local churches that made up the universal church. During their struggle with secular rulers from 1050 to 1300, however, the popes centralized control over the church and gave it the character of an absolute monarchy that it retains to our day.

The Papal Will to Power

What began with the Investiture Struggle was more than a struggle for control over the church. It also involved a struggle by popes for control over all Western society. It is important to look at that struggle again for two reasons. First, it shows that the popes' will to power, scarcely a gospel demand, extended far beyond the ecclesiastical realm. And second, during that struggle, constitutional principles were developed that should apply in today's church.

Near the beginning of that struggle stood a great reforming pope, Gregory VII (1073–1085). A year after his election, he made clear in a letter to Solomon, king of Hungary, that he did not intend to relinquish any temporal power the Roman see had acquired in previous feudal transactions. A year later (1075), the *Dictatus papae* was entered into Gregory's official register. Apart from claims concerning papal authority within the church, these are his claims in the civic realm:

8. That he [the pope] alone may use the imperial insignia.

9. That the pope is the only one whose feet are to be kissed by all princes.

12. That he may depose emperors.

17. That the pope may absolve subjects of unjust men from their fealty.

Gregory's best known display of power was to bring Emperor Henry IV to his knees in the snows at Canossa in January 1077.

Historians disagree in their assessment of Gregory. Was he a worldly prelate obsessed with desire to dominate Europe or a saintly servant of the church concerned only for the church's liberty and ecclesiastical reform? Tierney suggests that both may be true. Someone moved by an irresistible drive for power could be utterly convinced that everything he did was entirely for a cause greater than himself.[2] Perhaps the same judgment can be applied to other popes whose search for power we will discuss.

The papal struggle to prevent lay rulers from controlling the church continued in the conflict between the papacy and the Holy Roman emperors, as popes after Gregory VII sought to establish jurisdiction over secular rulers. A highly symbolic event had been Leo III's crowning of Charlemagne as emperor of the Romans on Christmas day in 800. Since the pope had crowned them emperors of Rome, it could hardly be denied that emperors should have some kind of authority in Rome. The popes, however, were not about to acknowledge the church of Rome as an imperial bishopric. The popes sought to solve their side of the problem by asserting that any rights the emperor possessed as Roman emperor came from the pope as the emperor's overlord. All through the twelfth century, popes tried to establish their dominion over emperors and, in fact, in 1133, Lothar III, on the occasion of his imperial coronation, did homage to the pope for some disputed land in Italy.

Frederick Barbarossa, however, made it quite clear, when he was crowned emperor by Pope Hadrian IV in 1155, that he claimed the imperial crown by right of conquest. Two years later, Hadrian wrote a letter to the emperor that seemed to contain the pope's claim to be the emperor's overlord. When Frederick reacted by threatening to invade Italy, Hadrian insisted that he had been misunderstood. Hadrian probably claimed lordship in deliberately ambiguous language. Had his claim gone unchallenged, it would have established a precedent. At the worst, his words could be explained away without too much loss of face.

No ambiguity, however, veiled the claims of Pope Innocent III (1198–1216) and Pope Innocent IV (1243–1254). They claimed both kingly and priestly power, basing their case on belief that Peter, the first pope, had received all power on earth from the Lord who was both king and priest. Innocent III insisted that, since Christ had established Peter and his successors as his vicars on earth, the pope should be the final court of appeal in all temporal cases. Since the pope had no army or other

---

[2] Brian Tierney, *The Crisis of Church & State 1050–1300* (Englewood Cliffs, N.J.: Prentice-Hall, 1964), pp. 46–51.

resources to enforce such a claim, however, Innocent introduced a useful, face-saving distinction, that is, that the pope was temporal overlord of all kings *de jure,* but not *de facto.*[3] Innocent held that in an ideal world, popes would be both, and if history worked out as it should, eventually they would be. But meanwhile popes could only exercise rightful jurisdiction over those kings who acknowledged their overlordship. John Lackland of England accepted his kingdom from the pope. Philip of France did not. Exercise of such claims against the emperors reached a climax when Pope Innocent IV deposed Frederick II at the Council of Lyons (1245). The Hohenstaufen dynasty was destroyed and, with it, the dream of a universal empire.

A Failed Theocracy

This set the stage for the papacy's next battle in its search for control over European political life. The struggle came between Philip IV, king of France, a rising national state, and Pope Boniface VIII.

In 1297, Philip forced Boniface to back down on the issue of clerical exemption from royal taxation. Four years later, Philip acted again to prove his mastery over his own kingdom. In a deliberately provocative act, he ordered a French bishop's arrest, trial in his own presence, and imprisonment on charges of blasphemy, heresy, and treason. To Boniface, the issue was not that the charges were false, but the king's gross presumption even to touch a bishop. He ordered all French bishops to attend a council in Rome to consider the state of religion in France. Philip forbade the bishops to attend. When the French bishops met in Rome in 1302, thanks to the king's prohibition only thirty-six out of seventy-eight appeared. A majority obeyed the king rather than the pope.

Boniface considered this an attack on the church's unity and promulgated *Unam sanctam,* the best known medieval document on spiritual and temporal power. It concluded with the famous statement:

---

[3] Brian Tierney, "The Continuity of Papal Political Theory in the Thirteenth Century: Some Methodological Considerations," *Medieval Studies* (Toronto), 27 (1965), pp. 238–239 (reprinted in *Church Law,* no. 5).

> We declare, state and define that it is altogether necessary
> for salvation for every human creature to be subject to the
> Roman Pontiff.[4]

The papal bull *Unam sanctam* is a long theological treatise on
the church's unity. Boniface saw clearly the threat to that unity
when bishops of a national hierarchy hesitated between allegiance to their king and obedience to the pope.[5] So much of
the document dealt with church unity that some modern commentators deny that it had political significance. Tierney is convinced, however, that passages in *Unam sanctam* claimed that
royal power was delegated to kings by the pope. Boniface's views
on papal authority probably did not differ from those of his predecessors. But these views had now been stated without ambiguity, in an official pronouncement that ended with a solemn
statement: to be saved every human being had to be subject to
the pope. This strong spiritual note ended what could easily be
interpreted as a political claim.

Philip's response was brutal. Nogaret, the king's minister,
left for Italy to settle the issue by force. The old pope, held
prisoner and abused for three days in his palace in Agani before being rescued by the townspeople, died a few weeks later.
In France, there seems to have been no wave of indignation,
even among the clergy. Pope Clement V (1305–1314), French
and completely dominated by Philip, denied that anything in
Unam sanctam was prejudicial to the French king or his kingdom. He wrote later that Philip and Boniface's other opponents
were guiltless and had "acted out of an estimable, just and sincere zeal and from fervor of their Catholic faith."[6]

In previous centuries, visions of a universal empire under
the ideal emperor had failed when emperors tried unsuccessfully to control the church. Now Boniface failed to realize Innocent III's dream of a universal society of peace and concord
in a united Christendom, led by the pope. Boniface's impatient
and irascible disposition and his preoccupation with his own
family's fortunes were certainly obstacles to attaining his goals.
But would a saintly pope have been more successful? Boniface

---

[4] *DS* 875.

[5] Brian Tierney, "Boniface VIII, Pope," *New Catholic Encyclopedia,* 2:672.

[6] Joseph R. Strayer, *On the Medieval Origins of the Modern State* (Princeton:
Princeton University Press, 1970), p. 56.

did not recognize that history had passed him by. New forces of nationalism in developing national states as well as principles of constitutional government, developed during these struggles, were incompatible with a united theocratic kingdom. Thus, the popes of the thirteenth century, successful at increasing auto- cratic, centralized control over the church, did not succeed in enforcing their claims in the secular sphere.

Canon Lawyers and Constitutional Democracy

The newly developing national states became the constitutional democracies of the modern world. Historically democracy has not been the customary way to organize political societies. Most past societies solved problems of maintaining order and unity in large and heterogeneous groups by concentrating spiritual and temporal power in one sacral ruler. Egyptian pharaohs, Peruvian Incas, and, until recently, Japanese emperors were all revered as divine beings. Roman Caesars bore the title *Pontifex maximus,* and early Christian martyrs paid with their lives for refusing to offer them incense. In the Eastern Roman empire, Christian emperors came close to achieving a similar spiritual role. They not only summoned the first great ecumenical church councils, but also completely dominated the church in their territories.

Tierney contends that a similar all-encompassing rule by one sacral ruler did not develop in the West because the Middle Ages always had at least two claimants to the role. On one side, an emperor or king claimed to rule as minister of God's authority on earth. On the other, the pope made the same claim as "vicar of Christ," one who takes Christ's place as both priest and king. Each opposing claimant possessed a formidable apparatus of government, and for several centuries neither could dominate the other completely. Over and over in daily life, people had to make decisions in conscience, or in self-interest, between these two conflicting appeals to their loyalty. Existence of two op- posing power structures, each demanding allegiance and neither able to dominate the other, greatly increased possibilities for human freedom.

Medieval canonists, in their struggle with these conflicting claims of authority for obedience and loyalty, combined the church's own principles and traditions, customary ideas of law from their Teutonic background, and the newly recovered Roman law to develop the constitutional ideas that are the foundation of contemporary democracies. Lord Acton wrote: "To that conflict of four hundred years we owe the rise of civil liberty."[7]

To understand how ideas of canon lawyers could so profoundly influence developments in secular government, we have to realize how closely ecclesiastical and secular systems intertwined. A comparison with conflicts between church and state in the modern world gives a false picture of medieval conflicts. In the church's struggle with totalitarian regimes today, the opposing institutions' leadership and bureaucracies are often radically polarized. By contrast, the personnel of the two medieval structures were being interchanged. In England, the king's chancellor was usually a bishop. When a historian like Strayer writes of the professionalism of chancery clerks and their essential role in building up medieval states, we have to realize that these clerks were "clerics" and that many were supported by benefices granted by the church. Indeed, churchmen were so deeply involved in secular politics that their political ideas and administrative techniques directly influenced lay governments. The interchange was especially important for development of constitutional ideas on representation and consent. These ideas usually emerged first in the writings of canon lawyers, who served in both royal chanceries and in the church's bureaucracy.

Roman Law and the Need for Consent

It is widely recognized that the revival of Roman law at Bologna around the year 1100 and Gratian's *Decretum* around 1140 had signal importance in the development we are describing. Into the fragmented feudal world, Roman law introduced ideas of strong government capable of legislating and taxing for the common good. Gratian's *Decretum* combined into one collection many ideas, church laws, and church practices from the whole of church history.

In the law school that developed at Bologna, decretists in their influential commentaries on the *Decretum* merged orderly principles of Roman law with complex and often contradictory evidence from church tradition. And in it all, they were in-

---

[7]Quoted in Brian Tierney, "Medieval Canon Law and Western Constitutionalism," *Church Law and Constitutional Thought in the Middle Ages*, no. 15.

fluenced by Teutonic customary law that tended to see law, not just as a ruler's command, but as an expression of a people's life. The decretists sought to provide a juridical basis for the ancient theological teaching that the church is the People of God, an ordered community of believers.[8]

If revived Roman law exalted the prince's authority and seemed to justify autocracy in the church, Gratian's *Decretum* recovered many democratic elements in the church's past. Texts revealed not only beliefs, but a community: early Christian life filled with community meetings, community sharing, community participation in decision making, and community elections. Above all there was a strong conviction that the consensus of the Christian people came from the active presence of the Holy Spirit at work in the church.

Indeed, despite centralized ecclesiastical power in Gratian's day, the church retained a structure of elected offices. Popes were elected by cardinals, and officials were elected in monasteries, cathedral chapters, collegiate churches, confraternities, universities, and new religious orders, notably the Dominicans with their influential constitution.

The nature of Gratian's collection of "discordant canons" protected the canonists from a non-historical orthodoxy. It revealed conflicting teachings, laws, and customs, and showed a thousand years of the church's history, warts and all.

The canonists applied to the pope Roman law's exalted description of a sovereign emperor, but they did so with examples of popes who had sinned and even fallen into heresy. A text of Gratian said that all popes were to be considered holy. Johannes Teutonicus commented around 1216: "Note, it does not say that they are holy but that they are presumed to be holy... which means until the contrary becomes apparent."[9]

The highly organized and centralized worldview of Roman law contrasted sharply with the canonists' own feuding, chaotic world and led them to face a perennial problem: how to concede to the ruler enough authority to govern effectively while safeguarding the community's right to protect itself against abuse of power. This was not an issue just in civil government nor was

---

[8]Brian Tierney, *Religion, Law and the Growth of Constitutional Thought, 1150–1650* (Cambridge: Cambridge University Press, 1982), p. 13.

[9]Tierney, "Medieval Canon Law and Western Constitutionalism," p. 9.

it simply a theoretical concern in the church. As papal power increased, unjust papal commands and exactions became a serious practical problem, often discussed in canonical writing. So even as canonists continued to exalt papal powers, they sought principles to temper papal authority. Writings of lawyers from the age of Innocent III contain the expected passages exalting papal power. But they also have sophisticated discussions of constitutional concepts: on representation and consent; and on necessary limits to lawful authority, including papal authority.

The canonists found their solution to the problem of papal authority, and its potential abuse, in the consensus of the entire Christian community. The indefectibility of the church guided by the Holy Spirit established norms of faith and order that could define limits of papal legislative and judicial powers.

Gratian had supplied a basis for their thinking with a text from Gregory the Great. Gregory taught that canons of the church's first four general councils were to be kept inviolate, because they had been established "by universal consent." The canonists built on the word "consent," quoting such phrases as "what touches all should be approved by all." On such notions they based the right of lay representation at general councils considering matters of faith. It was commonly held around 1200 that canons from general councils bound popes "in matters pertaining to faith and the general state of the church." Since popes usually presided at councils, this did not create a conflict between pope and council. An English canonist expressed the view "that the authority of a pope with a council is greater than that of a pope without one."[10] Hence, the pope acting together with a wide representation of the whole church was seen to have more authority than the pope acting alone.

Contrast this understanding with a question raised on the birth control issue after Vatican II. Was Paul VI bound by the decrees of Vatican II, which he had signed, or, as Archbishop Parente said to Bernard Häring, was he totally free to return to *Casti connubii?*

A clear statement on the importance of consent came from Hervaeus Natalis, professor of theology at the University of

---

[10]Pennington, *Pope and Bishops: The Papal Monarchy in the Twelfth and Thirteenth Centuries* (Philadelphia: University of Pennsylvania Press, 1984), p. 133.

Paris and Dominican master-general, who wrote around 1315 on the origin of jurisdiction. To the question "How is jurisdiction acquired?" Hervaeus answered: "Only by the consent of the people.... No community can be justly obliged except by its own consent or command of one having overlordship over it." Overlordship was *just,* however, only if the one who commanded had been justly appointed, and eventually it would be necessary to get back to someone whose authority was based on consent.[11]

But is not God the source of all authority? Paul wrote: "There is no authority except from God, and so whatever authorities exist have been appointed by God" (Rom. 13:1–2, NJB). But the practical problem is: how is God's authority transmitted? A solid theological tradition supports what is called the transmission theory.[12] According to this theory, God is the ultimate source of all authority. God's authority, however, is not transmitted directly to rulers, but indirectly through the people. Aquinas had already strongly implied this when he wrote:

> A law, properly speaking, regards first and foremost the order of the common good. Now to order anything to the common good belongs either to the whole people or to someone who is vicegerent [agent] of the whole people.[13]

The transmission theory was developed among Catholic theologians by Cajetan (d. 1534), Robert Bellarmine (d. 1621), and Suarez (d. 1617), the latter noted in the history of political theory for his opposition to the "divine right of kings," claimed by James I of England. The theory of the transmission of authority from God through the people is now accepted for every form of legitimate *civil* government. But official church teaching rejects the transmission theory for ecclesial offices. It insists that sacred power and a mandate for exercising it comes to the hierarchy from Christ and not through the people. Such a claim, at least in the period since the New Testament, is simply without foundation in verifiable historical fact.

---

[11]Tierney, *Religion, Law and the Growth of Constitutional Thought, 1150–1650,* pp. 44–46.

[12]Patrick Granfield, *Ecclesial Cybernetics: A Study of Democracy in the Church* (New York: Macmillan, 1973), pp. 179ff.

[13]*Summa theologiae,* I–II, 90, 3.

Hervaeus would have agreed, even for the office of the pope. Although the papal office had been established by God, God did not directly choose the officeholder. According to Hervaeus, the papacy was an elective office. The pope obtained his authority through election by the cardinals, and the cardinals acted for the entire Christian people, who had entrusted to them the function of election. So the pope also ruled by consent.[14] This was no revolutionary theory, but application to the fourteenth-century papacy of the ancient teaching of Leo I: "He who governs all should be elected by all." A twelfth-century canonist-bishop expressed it succinctly: "In these matters God is the bestower; we are His instruments."[15]

The Conscience of the People

Obedience, even to papal authority, was always subject to the rule of conscience. The great thirteenth-century canonist Hostiensis wrote:

If the subject cannot bring his conscience into conformity with his prelate's [which implicitly included the pope], then he should follow his conscience and not obey...even if his conscience is wrong.[16]

A famous case related to this issue involved the canon lawyer Pope Innocent IV, and Robert Grosseteste, bishop of Lincoln. In 1253, Grosseteste refused to confer a rich benefice on the pope's nephew. For Grosseteste, the many abuses in the bestowal of benefices were a churchwide scandal and, by his refusal, he obviously meant to make a public statement. He based his action on accepted canonical opinion of his day that no exercise of papal power should be endured that threatened the church's well-being. Canonists described such actions as "against the general state of the church" (*contra generalem statum ecclesiae*). Grosseteste claimed, adapting Paul's words in 2 Cor. 10:8, that the

---

[14]Tierney, *Religion, Law and the Growth of Constitutional Thought, 1150–1650*, p. 46.

[15]Quoted in "Roots of Western Constitutionalism in the Church's Own Tradition: The Significance of the Council of Constance," in James A. Coriden, ed., *We, the People of God: A Study of Constitutional Government in the Church* (Huntington, Ind.: Canon Law Society of America, 1968). pp. 117–118.

[16]Pennington, *Pope and Bishops*, p. 133.

pope's command had been not for building up the church but for its destruction.[17] Innocent IV's own writings contained justification for Grosseteste's action. In his *De sententia excommunicationis,* Innocent had indeed asserted that unjust papal commands must be obeyed, but Innocent himself then added a significant reservation, "unless the unjust command would vehemently disturb the state [peace and order] of the church (*statum ecclesiae*), or perhaps give rise to other difficulties."[18]

Let me suggest several present-day issues that seem to be more serious for the "state of the church" than awarding a rich benefice to the pope's nephew: muzzling of bishops who seek to discuss the ordination of women; deprivation for many of regular access to mass because there are too few priests, which is due largely to the drive to maintain the ecclesiastical discipline of celibacy; imposition of doubtful moral demands, as in condemnation of all use of artificial contraceptives or the discipline for the divorced and remarried; and silencing theologians who try to discuss such issues for the good of "the general state of the church."

The church's own traditions, derived from democratic elements in the church's past and developed by the church's own canonists, are a source of many of the constitutional principles underlying contemporary democracies. To adopt such constitutional practices into its own structure would not be to embrace an alien system, but to return to a tradition that initially drew its inspiration from the church, the work of great jurists who gave the medieval church its unified law.[19]

I contend that such structural changes are especially appropriate for a church in which all members receive the charisms of the Spirit and in which the guarantee of infallibility is to the whole church (*Lumen gentium,* no. 12). One of those charisms is the sense of the faithful, "*a faculty of perceiving the truth of the faith and of discerning anything opposed to it.*"[20] The peo-

---

[17]See Patrick Granfield, *The Limits of the Papacy: Authority and Autonomy in the Church* (New York: Crossroad, 1987), pp. 60–61.

[18]Brian Tierney, "Grosseteste and the Theory of Papal Sovereignty," *Church Law,* no. 6.

[19]Tierney, "Medieval Canon Law and Western Constitutionalism," p. 16.

[20]Yves M. Congar, "Towards a Catholic Synthesis," in Jürgen Moltmann and Hans Küng, *Who Speaks for the Church?* Concilium 148 (New York: Seabury, 1981), p. 74.

ple of God should be a primary source, a *locus theologicus,* of "what the Spirit is saying" to the church. Structures of constitutional democracy are best suited to make that source available to leaders in the church.

A Modern Parallel

We have examined a complex situation in which, during a struggle for control between popes and secular rulers, the church's lawyers developed constitutional principles that were gradually adopted in democratic states of the West. I would like to use a modern comparison to analyze the social and cultural context in which these events occurred.

The economist John Kenneth Galbraith has presented a description of contemporary dictatorships in undeveloped countries that resembles the situation in Europe in the Early Middle Ages.

> People who are subject in their daily lives to the personal authority or economic power of tribal leaders, large landowners or primal capitalists or the weight of economic depression are not especially sensitive to the authority of some civilian or military dictator or junta in some remote capital. Their freedom of expression is sufficiently circumscribed by the local talent, as also by poverty and an all-embracing struggle to survive. Mass illiteracy also contributes greatly to political docility.[21]

In Europe the barbarian invasions had brought an almost total collapse of Western society; most people were preoccupied with sheer physical survival. In fact "medieval conditions were essentially similar to those of an 'underdeveloped' society nowadays...."[22] As Galbraith points out, in undeveloped societies in the modern world

> all of this changes with economic and industrial development. The controlling circumstance then is simply that a

---

[21] John Kenneth Galbraith, "Economic Development: Engine of Democracy," *New York Times,* August 25, 1987.

[22] Brian Tierney and Sidney Painter, *Western Europe in the Middle Ages: 300–1475,* 3rd ed. (New York: Alfred A. Knopf, 1978), pp. 253–267.

very large number of people, individually and in organizations, insist on being heard. Poverty and ignorance have
sufficiently released their grip so as to allow the luxury —
in fact the imperative — of self-expression.

In the Early Middle Ages, chaotic conditions were gradually reversed at the end of the barbarian invasions. With return of
some kind of order, commerce revived and town life was restored. Traders and craftsmen obtained personal freedom that
they had not had as serfs attached to the soil. In towns, they
organized themselves into guilds and sought the right to man-
age their own fiscal and judicial affairs. They often developed
enough capital to offer money revenue to their lord in exchange
for privileges they wanted. Towns in the empire obtained charters that freed them from control of their local overlords. In
other areas, they freed themselves from control by local bishops.

Growth of towns created a market for agricultural products
that brought slow but significant changes in the life of the peas-
ants still on the land. Serfs could sell their surplus and offer
their lords tempting money payments for their freedom, or they
could escape to the towns. Town charters often provided that a
runaway serf who fled to a town and escaped capture for a year
and a day won freedom. In this same period, guilds of scholars
developed into the first universities, source of a growing educated class. Like merchant and craft guilds, the universities
struggled to become independent of both ecclesiastical and lay
authorities.

A development anticipating the feminist movement by many
centuries was the founding of the Beguines in the late twelfth
and early thirteenth centuries. These were religious communities in which unmarried women, mostly middle and upper
class, found an outlet for their idealism and emotional and social needs. In addition to their religious exercises, they sewed
for the poor, did baby sitting, and nursed the sick and needy.
Membership in beguinages released them from the usual inferior status of women. Some beguinages taught that women were
spiritual equals of men and allowed them to share religious authority and responsibility.[23] Release of important elements of

---

[23]Steven Ozment, *The Age of Reform, 1250–1550: An Intellectual and Re-*

the population from the grip of poverty and ignorance brought a widespread demand for freedom from arbitrary control. Availability of cheap reading material, with the invention of moveable type in the middle of the fifteenth century, increased literacy and the dissemination of knowledge and ideas.

These developments contributed to a climate similar to what Galbraith attributes to the effect of industrialization in modern society: "Poverty and ignorance have sufficiently released their grip so as to allow the luxury — in fact the imperative — of self-expression." In Europe an inflexible and often corrupt hierarchy failed to respond. The Reformation and the Enlightenment must be seen, in some measure, as results.

The church in France failed to read "the signs of the times." It continued its alliance with the *ancien régime* against a rising tide of democratic aspirations and thus helped prepare for the French Revolution. The church failed to recognize that the motto of the Revolution, "Liberty, Equality, Fraternity," represented gospel values.

Joseph Komonchak offers an excellent description of official Catholic reaction to the Revolution and the Napoleonic upheaval. He describes the building

of a new form of Catholicism as a counter-society autonomous and sovereign, centralized and bureaucratized, prizing clarity, order, and unity. The whole purpose of this new construction was anti-modern, designed to legitimate and render plausible a Catholic counterculture whose devotion and dogmas were an antidote to the spread of liberalism in economics, society, politics, and culture.[24]

The definition of papal infallibility in 1870 at Vatican I, biblical decrees and the anti-modernist crusade of Pius X (1903–1914), the encyclical letter *Humani generis* (1950) of Pius XII, and the

---

ligious History of Late Medieval and Reformation Europe (New Haven: Yale University Press, 1980), pp. 91–92. As James Brundage points out: "The reaction of the papacy was predictable: strenuous efforts to suppress the dissident women, accusations of heresy, intimations of sexual temptations and indiscretions and a strong papal injunction (from Boniface VIII) that *all* religious women must remain permanently cloistered (VI 3.16.1 *Periculoso*)." Letter to author.

[24]Joseph A. Komonchak, "Issues Behind the Curran Case: The Church & Modernity: From Defensiveness to Engagement," *Commonweal,* vol. 114, no. 2 (January 30, 1987), p. 44.

silencing of theologians, are all part of an effort to maintain
tight control over thought and conduct in the church. But, as
Galbraith pointed out in the political sphere, such a condition
cannot be maintained with an increasingly literate and econom-
ically liberated laity. Galbraith contends that the movement
toward democratization is historically inevitable.

I would suggest that, because of the distribution of "special graces among the faithful of every rank" (*Lumen gentium,*
no. 12), movement toward democratization should develop even
more inevitably in the church. Democratic structures are needed
if the church is to utilize the charism of the sense of the faithful as a source of theological insights. Vatican II taught: "The
whole body of the faithful who have an anointing that comes
from the holy one cannot err in matters of belief" (*Lumen gentium,* no. 12). Bishop Butler even suggested that, when the People of God do not accept what was intended as an *ex cathedra*
teaching, that would itself be sufficient evidence that the stringent conditions for infallible teaching had not been met.[25]

More than passive acceptance by the laity is involved, however. The laity must be heard because the Holy Spirit also speaks
through them. At the 1980 Synod on the Family, Cardinal Hume
spoke of the importance of listening to married people, the ones
who confer the sacrament of matrimony and also experience its
reality. But the laity have significant experience in many areas of life other than marriage. In his early condemnation of
liberation theology, Cardinal Ratzinger attempted to establish
a radical dichotomy between the secular and the "religious."[26]
But no aspect of reality is separated from the dominion of God,
and in many areas of that reality, the laity have experience and
insight.

As Vatican II teaches, the laity "shares also in Christ's prophetic office" (*Lumen gentium,* no. 12). Therefore the laity must
be recognized as part of the teaching church as well as part of
the learning church. Many bishops have come to recognize this,
as shown by the American bishops' wide consultation for their
pastoral letters on nuclear weapons, economics, and women's

---

[25]B. C. Butler, "Authority in the Church," *The Tablet,* vol. 231, no. 7141 (May 21, 1977), p. 479.

[26]See Juan Luis Segundo, S.J., *Theology and the Church: A Response to Cardi-
nal Ratzinger and a Warning to the Whole Church,* trans. John W. Diercksmeier (Minneapolis: Winston, 1985), pp. 27–29.

concerns in church and society. At the Synod on the Family many bishops presented points of view of the laity whom they had consulted. But consultation is not enough. The laity should be included as full-fledged members of the ecclesial bodies that make these decisions. "What touches all should be approved by all." In the medieval period the laity were present as active voting members of councils. A Synod on the Laity without fully active lay participants is a contradiction.

Intercommunion: Who Decides?

The question of intercommunion is a practical problem that exemplifies many of the issues we have discussed. Catholics who live in countries where most inhabitants have been baptized in the Roman Catholic church probably find it difficult to understand its practical significance. The present discipline is harsh: no communion for Catholics in non-Catholic churches and communion for non-Catholics in Catholic churches only if in grave spiritual need with no opportunity to receive in their own churches. This is often a painfully divisive issue: a source of embarrassment and division in family life and frustrating for groups gathered to promote Christian unity. This narrow official approval for the local level contrasts with the accord now achieved among theologians in dialogue on national and international levels. Roman Catholics have joined theologians from "virtually all confessional traditions" to produce a statement with "significant theological convergence...in doctrine and practice on baptism, eucharist and ministry."[27]

Vatican II opened the way for eucharistic reciprocity. In its encouragement of intercommunion, however, the council discriminated between separated churches of East and West on the basis of a too restrictive, although traditional, understanding of apostolic succession. Of the Eastern churches, the Decree on Ecumenism affirmed that because

> they possess true sacraments, above all — by apostolic succession — the priesthood and the Eucharist...some worship in common [*communicatio in sacris,* which involves

---

[27] *Baptism, Eucharist, and Ministry,* Faith and Order Paper 111 (Geneva: World Council of Churches, 1982), p. ix.

penance and anointing as well as the Eucharist] is not only
possible but is recommended.

(Unitatis redintegratio, no. 15)

Of the separated Western churches, the Decree on Ecumenism
asserted that "because of the lack of the sacrament of orders they
have not preserved the genuine and total reality of the Eucharistic mystery" (no. 22). Therefore, reciprocity is not allowed —
only individual communion in the Roman Catholic church for
separated Western Christians in grave spiritual need.[28]

Further studies in history and scripture have seriously eroded
the basis for this distinction between the separated churches of
East and West. Roman Catholic participants in the national
Lutheran-Catholic dialogue stated that they found serious defects in arguments brought against the validity of the Lutheran
churches' eucharistic ministry. They said, "we see no persuasive
reason to deny the possibility of the Roman Catholic church rec-
ognizing the validity of this Ministry... and, correspondingly
the presence of the body and blood of Christ in the eucharistic celebrations of the Lutheran churches."[29] As for Anglican
orders, Roman Catholic historian John Jay Hughes writes that
four centuries of attacks on the validity of Anglican orders are
a history of constant defeats and changes of front. One could
defend Anglican orders out of quotations from attackers admit-
ting that, on this or that point, the Anglican case is sound.[30]
Within the framework of the traditional understanding of a tactile chain of succession from the apostles, that is, the laying on
of the hands, we should recognize that Lutherans and Anglicans
have valid orders and, therefore, the real presence of the body
and blood of Christ in their eucharistic celebrations. Eucharistic reciprocity should be as acceptable with them as with the
Orthodox.

What of the Eucharist in churches that celebrate the Lord's
Supper but do not claim a tradition of tactile succession? Current biblical studies undermine the chain theory of apostolic

---

[28] As for the Orthodox, the Standing Conference of the American Orthodox
Bishops has rejected the possibility of intercommunion with Roman Catholics.

[29] "Reflections of the Roman Catholic Participants," *Lutherans and Catholic
in Dialogue IV* (1970), p. 32.

[30] John Jay Hughes, *Stewards of the Lord: A Reappraisal of Anglican Orders*
(London: Sheed & Ward, 1970), p. 287.

succession on which the need for tactile succession is based. A beginning for the chain is missing. No evidence exists acceptable to reputable scripture scholars either that Jesus ordained anyone or that the "Twelve" who were present at the Last Supper appointed and ordained their successors.[31] In light of the teaching of Vatican II on ecclesiology, baptism, presence, theology, and the church's teaching on extraordinary ministers, a strong case exists for the real presence of Christ in eucharistic celebrations of churches with no claim to a tactile succession.[32]

Surely Cardinal Johannes Willebrands, president of the Vatican Secretariat for Promoting Christian Unity, understood all the important background issues when at the 1980 Synod on the Family he suggested that to promote unity in the family the time had come to study the possibility of eucharistic reciprocity: that is, the non-Catholic spouses receive communion in the Catholic church and Catholic spouses receive the Eucharist in another church.[33] His suggestion, however, was ignored.

Five years later Pope John Paul II rejected the request for intercommunion made by nine U.S. Lutheran bishops visiting the Vatican:

> There is joy and hope, because the Lutheran-Catholic dialogue over the last 20 years has made us increasingly aware of how close we are to each other in many things that are basic. We experience sorrow, too, because there are important issues which still divide us in the profession of faith, preventing us from celebrating the Eucharist together.[34]

Willebrands seems not to have considered these "important issues" as obstacles to reciprocity for the good of family unity.

---

[31] Raymond E. Brown, *Priest and Bishop: Biblical Reflections* (New York: Paulist, 1970), pp. 47–86; "Difficulties in Using the New Testament in American Catholic Discussions," *Louvain Studies* 6 (1976), pp. 144–158; "*Episkope* and *Episkopos:* The New Testament Evidence," *Theological Studies,* vol. 41, no. 2 (June 1980), p. 332.

[32] See my article "Intercommunion and Union," *Journal of Ecumenical Studies,* vol. 22, no. 3 (Summer 1985), pp. 594–603.

[33] Jan Grootaers and Joseph A. Selling, *The 1980 Synod of Bishops "On the Role of the Family": Exposition of the Event and an Analysis of Its Texts,* Bibliotheca Ephemeridum Theologicarum Lovaniensium (Leuven: Leuven University Press, 1983), p. 102.

[34] Vatican City (NC), *Catholic Bulletin,* October 6–12, 1985.

In his history of paragraph 8 of the Decree on Ecumenism, George Tavard, a member of Vatican II's Theological Commission, noted that the text, "in keeping with the present structure of authority in the Catholic Church," refers the decision on appropriateness of intercommunion to the local bishop, the episcopal conference, and the bishop of Rome.[35]

Is only the hierarchy qualified to make a judgment in this matter? Is this not an area in which the *sensus fidelium,* the sense of the faithful, is as significant as that of the hierarchy? Here again do we not see the Roman magisterium imposing its view as if it were the only legitimate position — notwithstanding "probable opinion" to the contrary? Many Catholics, intelligent and deeply committed, have begun to practice intercommunion against expressed prohibitions of officialdom. For them, this is not a matter of indifferentism, so much feared by the hierarchy. These Catholics are convinced this is the way the Spirit is at work in the church. They are aware of the high level of agreement reached among Christian churches in official discussions. They sense that remaining differences with other Christians are not sufficient to justify the present radical institutional divisions. They certainly do not consider these differences important enough to cause division at the Lord's table.

Certainly, many who practice intercommunion see it as a means of strengthening the bonds within their families and of breaking down unnecessary barriers to the union for which the Lord of the church prayed. The Spirit's gift of newness usually manifests itself first at the grassroots, in the sense of the faithful. The hierarchy's usual role is "to distinguish between spirits" (1 Cor. 12:10), without quenching the Spirit (1 Thess. 5:19).

Vox populi, vox Dei. For internal church issues this "voice of God" would be made manifest through the sense of the faithful, the *sensus fidelium.* That may have been difficult to determine in past ages with poor means of communication, but in our day reliable and competently conducted surveys can inform us about what the faithful believe and what they reject as contrary to their faith experience. A wise church leadership will start to use this valuable tool.

---

[35] George H. Tavard, A.A., "Praying Together: *Communicatio in Sacris* in the Decree on Ecumenism," in Dom Alberic Stacpoole, O.S.B., *Vatican II Revisited by Those Who Were There* (Minneapolis: Winston, 1986), p. 214.

The American Contribution

If democracy is the future of the church, do American Catholics with their experience of democracy and pluralism have a special role to play in the church? In his address to Pope John Paul at the meeting with the American bishops in Los Angeles, Cardinal Bernardin said:

> The church in the United States has much to contribute to the universal church. I am thinking, for example, of our role in the development of the documents on religious liberty and ecumenism of the Second Vatican Council.[36]

It is widely recognized that John Courtney Murray's American background played a major part in his important contribution to Vatican II's Declaration on Religious Liberty, *Dignitatis humanae.*

Democracy and pluralism will be essential in a united church in the future. The churches of the East have always recognized the bishop of Rome as the first among equals. Lutherans and Anglicans in the official dialogues recognize the need for a ministry for the unity of the whole church, and they acknowledge that the bishop of Rome has traditionally held that position in the church. But reunion is not possible as long as they perceive the style of governance in Rome to be contrary to the spirit of the gospels.

A united church of the future should be democratic and it will have to be a community of very diverse churches. Rome's experience with the Eastern rites within the Roman Catholic church is enlightening. There was a serious move to Latinize these churches as part of an effort to construct, in Komonchak's words, "a new form of Catholicism as a counter-society autonomous and sovereign, centralized and bureaucratized, prizing clarity, order, and unity." Abandonment of that tragic effort is a good omen for the future.

Galbraith says that "we have heard too little of its [democracy's] practical utility, and, more especially, given the relevant circumstances, of its historical inevitability." If democracy is both useful and inevitable, then the experience of how to live

---

[36]*Origins,* vol. 17, no. 16 (October 1, 1987), p. 256.

democratically in a pluralistic society may be the special contribution of the American church to the church of the future.

For individual believers, one's conscience is, in Newman's words, "a sacred and sovereign monitor." Catholics have a right to that "other information" of which Häring speaks, to dissenting "probable opinion," to form enlightened consciences on issues we have examined here. To deny that right is immoral. It will be said that the attempt to close ranks by imposing doubtful teaching is done in good faith for God's honor and the preservation of the unity of the holy church. This good faith produced the Syllabus of Errors of Pius IX, the biblical decrees of Pius X, the silencing of scholars such as Teilhard de Chardin, John Courtney Murray, Yves Congar, and others for their teaching on such subjects as evolution and the separation of church and state. To that list of scholars must now be added Charles E. Curran, who, among American theologians, led the original criticism of *Humanae vitae.*

Harm done by an autocratic official teaching where decisions of conscience are involved is especially serious: imposing excessive moral burdens on those trying to please God; causing guilt among those unable to meet the rigorous demands of what are essentially doubtful laws; estranging many from the church; placing serious obstacles in the way of the reunion of the churches; undermining the credibility of a magisterium to which Catholics should be able to listen with reverent confidence. In our day of mass communications and a well-educated laity, only a voice that is recognized as completely open and honest will be trusted. That trusted voice will not be autocratic and authoritarian; it will relish a diversity of "probable opinions" because it knows that the many voices of the people can only enrich the magisterium.

And the Catholic sincerely following a probable opinion opposed to official teaching . . . remains a faithful Catholic.

Glossary

anathema: a formal ecclesiastical curse involving excommunication, sometimes added to conciliar decrees.

annulment: declaration by a church court that an apparent marriage has not been valid.

benefice: an ecclesiastical office to which the revenue from an endowment is attached.

canon law: the ecclesiastical law governing the church.

Casti connubii: Pope Pius XI's encyclical on marriage.

charism: an extraordinary power given by the Holy Spirit for the good of the church.

Christian Family Movement (CFM): a lay movement of married Catholics involved in Catholic Action.

Congregation for the Doctrine of the Faith (CDF): a Vatican administrative organ of church government, successor to the Holy Office, which succeeded the Holy Inquisition.

curia: the body of congregations, tribunals, and offices through which the pope governs the church.

decretal: a papal letter giving an authoritative decision on a point of canon law.

decretist: medieval canon lawyer; commentator on Gratian's *Decretum.*

de fide: said of a teaching that must be believed as a matter of faith.

defined doctrine: a doctrine that a pope or council requires to be accepted as a matter of faith.

deposit of faith: God's revelation in scripture.

dissent: difference of opinion, disagreement with undefined teaching.

doctrine: a teaching from an official church source.

dogma: a doctrine infallibly taught.

encyclical: a papal letter usually addressed to the bishops of the world.

ex cathedra: "from the chair"; highest level of papal teaching.

extraordinary magisterium: church teaching at the highest formal level by pope or council.

Gaudium et spes: Vatican Council II's "Constitution on the Church in the Modern World" (1965).

heresy: adherence to a religious opinion contrary to church dogma.

Humani generis: Pope Pius XII's encyclical enhancing the authority of papal teaching in encyclicals (1950).

Humanae vitae: Pope Paul VI's encyclical letter condemning all use of artificial contraception (1968).

indifferentism: belief that all religions are equally valid.

infallibility: ability to teach without possibility of error in (1) solemn conciliar definitions, (2) *ex cathedra* teaching by popes and (3) teaching of the ordinary and universal magisterium of bishops in union with the pope (*Lumen gentium*, no. 25).

Lumen gentium: Vatican Council II's "Constitution on the Church" (1964).

magisterium: official teaching office in the church, especially of the pope and bishops.

Melkite-rite: a branch of the church in union with Rome which has a married clergy; one of several Eastern-rite churches.

metropolitan: an archbishop, head of a province that includes several dioceses.

natural law: a body of law derived from nature and binding on human society apart from or in addition to positive law.

ordinary and universal magisterium: teaching of all the bishops in unanimous agreement with the pope.

papal bull: a solemn papal letter usually sealed with a lead seal (bulla).

Pastor aeternus: Vatican Council I's constitution containing the definition of papal infallibility.

penitential: a book listing penances to be imposed for particular sins.

personalism: a doctrine emphasizing the significance, uniqueness, and inviolability of the person.

probabiliorism: the moral system according to which, in a doubt of conscience concerning the morality of a certain course of conduct, one must follow the more probable opinion.

probabilism: the moral system according to which in a doubt of conscience about the morality of a particular course of conduct, a person may lawfully follow the opinion for liberty, provided it is truly probable, even though the opinion for law is definitely more probable.

schema: a document proposed for consideration at Vatican Council II.

sensus fidelium* or *sensus fidei: sense of the faithful, understood as the people of God's perception of truth as they are guided by the gifts of the Holy Spirit.

Stoicism: a philosophy that held that the wise repressed emotion and were indifferent to pleasure or pain.

suffragan: a diocesan bishop subordinate to a metropolitan.

Synod of Bishops: a meeting at regular intervals of some of the bishops from around the world called by the pope to consider special issues in the life of the church.

synoptic gospels: Matthew, Mark, and Luke.

Tuas libenter: also knows as "the Munich brief"; Pius IX's letter to the archbishop of Munich that contains the first reference in a church document to the teaching of the "ordinary magisterium."

Index

167

Abbreviations

AAS   *Acta Apostolicae Sedis*

CCSL   *Corpus Christianorum, Series Latina.* Tournhold: Brepols, 1954.

CSEL   *Corpus Scriptorum ecclesiasticorum Latinorum.* Vienna: F. Tempsky, 1866–.

D   Denzinger, H. J. *Enchiridion Symbolorum, definitiorum et declarationum.* Freiburg: Herder, 1953.

DS   Denzinger, H. J., and A. Schönmetzer. *Enchiridion Symbolorum et Definitionem.* Barcelona: Herder, 1965.

GCS   *Die greichischen christlichen Schriftsteller der Ersten Drie Jahrhunderte.* Leipzig: J. C. Hinrichs, 1897–.

Mansi   *Sacrorum conciliorum nova et amplissima collectio.* Ed. Giovanni Domenico Mansi. 60 vols. Paris: Hubert Welter, 1901–1927.

PG   *Patrologiae cursus completus...series Graeca.* Ed. J. P. Migne. 167 vols. Paris: J. P. Migne, 1844–1864.

PL   *Patrologiae cursus completus...series Latina.* Ed. J. P. Migne. 221 vols. Paris: J. P. Migne, 1844–1864.

Critical Comments on *Why You Can Disagree...*
and Remain a Faithful Catholic

"Fr. Kaufman's book is a carefully reasoned and balanced presentation of a subtle and complex argument. His position on controversial issues in the church is one with which many laity already agree completely and which the clergy and the hierarchy cannot afford to ignore. The book demands careful and serious reading." — **Andrew Greeley, University of Chicago**

"Fr. Kaufman has written an important book for Catholics who take their faith seriously. By encouraging us to develop an informed conscience he proves himself a reliable defender of genuine authority. *Why You Can Disagree...* should help thousands of lay people to discover that theology affects their everyday lives and is too serious to be left exclusively to specialists." — **Joseph Cunneen, Editor, *Cross Currents***

"This book is a rigorous, objective, unrelenting inquiry and report on the church's teaching on critical and controversial moral and theological issues of the past, leading to judgment on comparable issues in the present.

"This book should be required reading for all bishops, priests, and other persons concerned with defining what is to be believed, rejecting what is not to be believed, and challenging what is 'in between.'" — **Eugene J. McCarthy**

"Fr. Kaufman writes with the freshness and audacity of a young man in love — with the church. Readers will have to marvel, then, to learn that this scholarly Benedictine was born in 1911. Catholics might consider giving this holy and hopeful book to friends who say they have 'fallen away' because they couldn't buy all the church's 'certain teachings' on birth control or on divorce and remarriage. As Father Kaufman reviews those teachings, we begin to see that they're not certain. And, as he says, since the people of God haven't 'received' them, they're hardly even 'teachings' either. I like the unspoken corollary of all this:

those who've fallen away ought to consider falling back in —
with young whippersnappers like Fr. Kaufman."
— **Robert Blair Kaiser, author of**
The Politics of Sex and Religion

"A valuable book that should be read by Catholics. The chapters on the Birth Control Commission tell a story that must be told." — **Patty Crowley**

"Philip Kaufman makes a convincing case for conscientious dissent from official teaching — a happy combination of in-depth research and reasoning which insists on the right of the People of God to know." — **Edward S. Skillin,** *Commonweal*

"A Catholic's conscience faced with today's difficult and distressing religious issues needs to be informed — of God's will, the church's teachings, theological opinions, the facts of history, and the facts of life. Philip Kaufman's book — based on the author's profound understanding of controversies as complex as birth control, divorce, and infallibility — will be immensely informative and helpful to Catholics troubled by moral and doctrinal conundrums.

"Fr. Kaufman's presentation of the most troublesome subjects is thoughtful and lucid. For Catholics who think and worry and think again; for parents who want a responsible book to discuss with their adult children; and for those who labor under the illusion that the hard questions have easy answers, *Why You Can Disagree...* will be indispensable."
— **Robert L. Spaeth, author of**
The Church and a Catholic's Conscience